Giuliano Iantorno / M

SECOND EDIT

TURNING POINTS 3
COMMUNICATING IN ENGLISH

ADDISON-WESLEY PUBLISHING COMPANY

Reading, Massachusetts • Menlo Park, California • New York • Don, Mills, Ontario
Wokingham, England • Amsterdam • Bonn • Sydney • Singapore • Tokyo • Madrid
San Juan • Paris • Seoul • Milan • Mexico City • Taipei

A Publication of the ESL Publishing Group

Project Director: Kathleen Sands Boehmer

Production/Manufacturing: James W. Gibbons

Permissions: Sheila Spinney

Photo Research: Karen Howse

Consultants:
Robert Saitz   Charles Skidmore

Design, production, and illustration provided by Publishers' Graphics, Inc., Bethel, Connecticut.
Illustrators: Eulala Connor, Joel Snyder, Kathie Kelleher, Ethel Gold, Tom Garcia, Ex Libris, PC&F, Inc., Janet Muller
Cover design by Marshall Henrichs

Copyright © 1994, 1989, 1986 by Addison-Wesley Publishing Company, Inc. This work is based in part on *Communication Tasks*, copyright © 1982 by Nicola Zanichelli, S.p.A. All rights reserved. No part of this publication may be reproduced, stored in a retrieval system, or transmitted in any form or by any means, electronic, mechanical, photocopying, recording, or otherwise, without the prior written permission of the publisher.
Printed in the United States of America.

ISBN 0-201-53822-9
2 3 4 5 6 7 8 9 10 – WC – 98 97 96 95

CONTENTS

1 CREATURES FROM OUTER SPACE 1
Talk about unexpected events
Describe a scene
Let's Rock! *Feelings and Emotions*

simple past • *past progressive*
while clauses • there is/are/was/were
predicate adjectives • on the right/left
verbs: began, broke, bought, heard, rang

2 VACATION SLIDES 7
Make guesses • Agree or disagree
Locate and identify people
Let's Rock! *Going on Vacation*
POEM: *Nolan Davis* (Mel Glenn)

demonstrative pronouns this/that
verb *defined* • *pronouns* one/ones
possessive adjectives • *adverbs of frequency*
prepositions in front of, next to

3 CAMPING IN THE WEST 14
Locate people and things
Identify people's possessions

negative questions • noun *defined*
possessive 's/s' • Whose?
preposition *defined* • *verb:* thought

4 WHEN'S YOUR BIRTHDAY? 23
Ask and talk about dates
Ask and talk about birthdays
Ask and talk about past and future events
Identify people's clothing

future going to • *future real conditional*
What? When? *(dates)* • pronoun *defined*
demonstrative adjectives this/that/these/those

5 CAN I HELP YOU? 30
Ask and talk about heights
Make comparisons
Ask and talk about age and height
Make a choice
Let's Rock! *Over and Over Again*
POEM: *In the Sun* (Lilian Moore)

would like/would rather • can/could
some/a lot/any • count/non-count nouns
comparison of adjectives • conjunction since
verbs: grew/grown

6 GOING TO A CONCERT 38
Express preferences • Make comparisons
Agree or disagree

like/love + gerund • preposition by
Which? • irregular comparative, superlative
Why/Because • So can/do I • adjective defined

7 THE BEST SINGER 45
Express opinions
POEM: *Crystal Rowe* (Mel Glenn)

superlative -est, most • verb: won
conjunctions and, but, so, in fact

8 BREAKFAST IS READY! 54
Offer and accept or refuse food
Express preferences • Agree or disagree
Let's Rock! *Street Beat*

How about? What about?
indefinite pronouns anything, nothing,
anyone, anywhere • adverb defined

9 BACK TO SCHOOL 62
Ask and talk about quantity
Identify people and places
Let's Rock! *Busy, Busy, Busy*

relative defining clauses: who/that
How much?/How many? • verb: wrote

10 WHERE SHOULD WE GO? 70
Ask for and give suggestions • Agree or disagree
Let's Rock! *No, No, No*

Let's + verb • should

11 AN INVITATION 77
Report what people are asking
Report what people are saying
Report people's commands and requests

if clauses • reported speech
verb: wrote

12 MAKING ARRANGEMENTS 86
Ask and talk about past events
Invite people • Arrange to meet people
Ask for and give information
Let's Rock! *Weekend*

object pronouns • reflexive pronouns
verb: cut (past)

13 AT THE SCIENCE EXHIBIT 95
Express opinions • Express preferences
Agree or disagree

Neither can/do/did/am (etc.)

14 A TRIP TO THE RACES 103
Ask and talk about your experiences
Ask and talk about time

present perfect • adverb there
verbs: was/were/been

15 TAKING THE BUS 110
Ask and talk about recent activities

verbs: did/done, ate/eaten, went/gone,
read/read, saw/seen, wrote/written

16 NELL'S VICTORY 115
Ask and talk about people's lives
Ask and talk about past habits
Let's Rock! *Rock and Roll Baby*

present perfect progressive
past habitual: used to • since/for + time
verbs: drank/drunk, drove/driven, spoke/spoken

LET'S ROCK!: SONG LYRICS 123

WORDS AND EXPRESSIONS 133

APPENDIX 137

CREATURES FROM OUTER SPACE

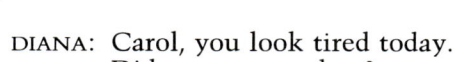

DIANA: Carol, you look tired today. Did you stay up late?
CAROL: Yes. I saw *Creatures from the Black Hole*, the new movie with Chris Lyons.
DIANA: He's so cute! Tell me, what was it about?
CAROL: Well, the first scene was out in the country. There were only a few lights from houses, and there was a small farmhouse on the right. It was so quiet and spooky. Suddenly this huge glowing light started to come down from the sky.
DIANA: The spaceship!
CAROL: Right. And while it was coming down, its lights flashed in millions of colors and there was a loud noise like thunder.
DIANA: I bet you were scared!
CAROL: I sure was! Then the door of the spaceship opened and about a dozen creatures came out.
DIANA: Wow! What did they do next?
CAROL: Well, while they were looking around, the farmer and his wife opened the door of their house and . . .

Class bell rings.

DIANA: Oh, wait! You'll have to tell me the rest later. I have to go to class.
CAROL: Okay. I'll tell you at lunch.
DIANA: Don't forget! See you later.
CAROL: Bye!

Communication Points

Talk about unexpected events

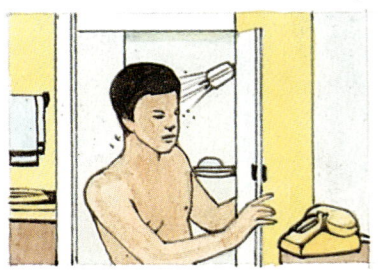  

a. taking a shower/
   telephone rang

b. exercising/
   broke my glasses

c. jogging/
   it began to rain

d. sleeping/
   heard a scream

e. watching TV/
   power went off

f. eating/
   saw a bug in my soup

Ask and answer with your partner. Use *happy*, *sad*, *excited*, *worried*, *scared*, or *mad*.

> A: While I was taking a shower, the telephone rang.
> B: I bet you were mad.
> A: I sure was.

Describe a scene

1. Describe the scene below. Work with your partner.

> There is a woman walking. On the right, there is a bus stop.

2. Now close your book and describe what you saw in the picture. Work with your partner.

There was . . . .

2 UNIT ONE

3. Pretend you took the "photos" below while you were on vacation. Describe one of them to your partner, using *There is/are* . . . . *On the right/left* . . . . Your partner will guess which one it is. Then change roles.

a.

b.

c.

d.

4. Choose one of the pictures. Then close your book and describe it to your partner, using *There was/were* . . . . Your partner will look in the book and try to guess which picture you are describing. Then change roles.

Language Points
Listening

Look at the picture below and listen to the description. On your paper, write three things in the picture that do not match the description you hear.

CREATURES FROM OUTER SPACE 3

Reading about geography
THE DISAPPEARING RAIN FORESTS

1. One of the most alarming facts in recent history is the rapid disappearance of the world's rain forests. Researchers have estimated that a typical four square mile area of a rain forest contains 125 different animals, 150 species of butterflies, 400 kinds of birds, and 750 different kinds of trees. Rain forests also supply mankind with a variety of important foods and medicines.

2. Unfortunately, much of the land in the rain forest countries, especially in South America, has been sold and continues to be sold to large lumber companies. These lumber companies want the land so that they can obtain hardwood for the construction industry. Many scientists believe that when the wildlife leaves the area, they may not flourish elsewhere.

3. Another reason behind the disappearance of the rain forests is the emphasis on expanding the agriculture of the area. Many people move from large cities to the rain forests in order to be farmers. They build small homes there and clear the land. They are called slash and burn farmers because they burn all the trees that they don't want or need. However, the soil in the rain forest is very thin. After a few years the tropical rains wash away all of the good nutrients in the soil and people can't continue to plant crops. Then these farmers have to move on—farther into the forest, leaving behind totally useless land.

4. The destruction doesn't end there either. Floods occur in the valleys below the wasteland. Heavy rains make the land slide downhill. Before the trees were cut down, rain would water the vegetation in the forest. Now the rain poses many severe problems.

5. Rain forests are clearly in trouble. They are disappearing at nearly 50 acres per minute. Perhaps it's not too late to help though. People all over the world are involved in efforts to help stop further destruction. Average citizens are learning more and more about the importance of the rain forests. They're learning to conserve and to think globally. There is hope that rain forests will still be on this earth for our children's children.

> **GLOSSARY**
> a·**larm**·ing—disturbing
> **spe**·cies—smallest group in which animals and plants can be divided or sorted
> **lum**·ber—wood
> **flour**·ish—grow well
> **ag**·ri·**cul**·ture—farming

1. **Copy and complete the sentences, using one of the words or phrases from the glossary.**
   a. It is an . . . fact that the rain forests are disappearing.
   b. Some wildlife may not . . . when they move away from an area.
   c. . . . companies cut down trees for hardwood.
   d. Over one hundred different . . . of butterflies live in the rain forest.
   e. People have moved to the rain forest to expand the . . . of the area.
   f. It is important to . . . and take care of the earth.

2. **Scanning is reading quickly for specific information. Scan the passage quickly to find the topics below. Then write on your paper the number of the paragraph where you can find the information.**
   a. slash and burn farmers
   b. disappearance of rain forests
   c. floods in the valleys
   d. learning to conserve
   e. expansion of agriculture

3. **A fact is something you can check or prove. An opinion is something that someone thinks or believes, but that cannot be checked or proved. Look at the following statements and decide which ones are fact and which ones are opinion. Write the letter and *fact* or *opinion* on your paper. Then discuss your answers with your partner.**
   a. Rain forests supply the world with food and medicine.
   b. Farmers don't want the wildlife in the rain forest.
   c. Rain forests are disappearing rapidly.
   d. Lumber companies don't want to conserve the rain forests.
   e. Heavy rains cause problems in the rain forests.

Practice Points

1. **Copy the sentences and fill in the blanks. Use *There was/There were*. Don't forget your capitalization and punctuation.**
   a. . . . a lake in the postcard picture.
   b. . . . a horror movie on TV.
   c. . . . two men fishing.
   d. . . . a woman waterskiing.
   e. . . . two sisters crossing the street.
   f. . . . many children on the beach.
   g. . . . a woman sitting in the sun.
   h. . . . a bug in my salad.
   i. . . . some boys skating on the sidewalk.

2. **Write questions about the underlined words. Use *When, Where, What,* or *Who*. The first one is done for you.**
   a. . . . ? I went to Puerto Rico.   *Where did you go?*
   b. . . . ? She bought a new dress.
   c. . . . ? I went to Paris last summer.
   d. . . . ? They got up at seven.
   e. . . . ? She saw her grandmother.
   f. . . . ? I ate a sandwich for lunch.
   g. . . . ? I called Sarah last night.
   h. . . . ? I got a stereo for my birthday.
   i. . . . ? Carol went to the playground.

3. **Look at the pictures at the top of page 2. Write a dialogue for each one, following the example given for picture a.**

4. Write a letter to a friend. Describe a place you visited on vacation last year. If you didn't go on vacation, describe a place from your imagination! Remember to indent the first line of each paragraph, as in the example.

> Dear Marie,
> Hi. How are you? Did you go anywhere for your summer vacation? I went to....

Let's Rock!

Turn to page 124.
Listen to the song *Feelings and Emotions*.
Read the words as you listen. Then sing along!

Check Points

Communication Points

Talk about unexpected events — While I was taking a shower, the telephone rang.
Describe a scene — There is a woman walking.
On the right, there is a bus stop.

1.
While	I was we were	taking a shower, watching TV, jogging,	the telephone rang. the power went off. it began to rain.

2.
I bet you were	mad. scared. angry.

3.
| On the right,
On the left, | there is a woman walking.
there are houses. |
| | there was a woman walking.
there were houses. |

Words and Expressions

begin	excited	new	shower	I bet
birthday	exercise	playground	sidewalk	I sure was
boys	happy	power	sun	last night
break	hear	ring	waterskiing	last summer
bug	mad	scared	while	went off
cross	many	scream	worried	

Present	Past
begin	began
break	broke
buy	bought
hear	heard
ring	rang

6 UNIT ONE

2 VACATION SLIDES

BILL: It's raining *again!* What are we going to do?
TIM: Bill and Carol, why don't you show us your vacation slides?
BILL: Do you really want to see them?
JANET: Sure we do. We hardly ever have a chance to see them. Come on, John—help me put up the screen.
BILL: Okay, here we go. This first slide is in Colorado, where my Uncle Jim lives.
JOHN: Wow, look at those mountains! Who are the two men next to the tent?
CAROL: The one on the right is Uncle Jim, and of course, the other one is my dad. Next . . .
JANET: I know where this is—Los Angeles.
BILL: Nope. That's San Francisco. We went there with Uncle Jim and his family. The kids on the left are my cousins.
TIM: Disneyland!
CAROL: Uh huh. The woman on my left is Aunt Judy.
JOHN: Oh, that must be the Grand Canyon in Arizona.
BILL: Right again. We rode on donkeys, all the way to the bottom. See me, standing next to that donkey?
CAROL: And now this must be . . .
MR. DAY: Anybody for a snack?
BILL: Great idea, Dad. Let's take a break.

Communication Points

Make guesses
Agree or disagree

1. Which of the photos are from Carol and Bill's trip? Where do you think the other ones were taken? Write your guesses on a piece of paper.

a.

b.

c.

d.

e.

f.

2. Now practice with your partner like this. Change roles.

> A: Look at picture *a*. That must be New York.
> B: That's right. That's the Empire State Building, and it's in New York.
> A: Picture *b*. I think that's Los Angeles.
> B: No, you're wrong. That's the Golden Gate Bridge, and it's in San Francisco.

Answers:
a. Empire State Building, New York b. Golden Gate Bridge, San Francisco c. Eiffel Tower, Paris, France. d. Grand Canyon, Arizona e. Colosseum, Rome, Italy. f. Swiss Alps, Switzerland.

Locate and identify people

1. Read these sentences.

John Bill

Mrs. Day Miss Bennett

a. There are two boys at the bus stop. The one on the right is Bill. The other one is John.

b. You can see two women in the yard. The one on the left is Mrs. Day. The other one is Miss Bennett.

2. Find the sentences that go with each picture and complete them correctly.

Mr. Day Mrs. Day

Bob Ken Bill

Tim Diana

John Janet

a. You can see two people on High Street. The one on the . . . is John. The other one is . . . .
c. There are . . . boys in the living room. The one on the . . . is Bill.

b. There are two people on Oak Avenue. The one on the left is . . . . The other one is . . . .
d. There are two people in the store. The one on the left is . . . . The . . . one is . . . .

3. Look at the pictures in exercises 1 and 2. Then ask and answer with your partner.

> A: Who are the two boys at the bus stop?
> B: The one on the right is Bill. The other one is John.

VACATION SLIDES

Language Points
Reading advertisements

A COAST TO COAST TOUR
NEW YORK   ST. LOUIS   DENVER   PHOENIX   GRAND CANYON   SAN FRANCISCO

15 Days from $1200, inclusive from NEW YORK

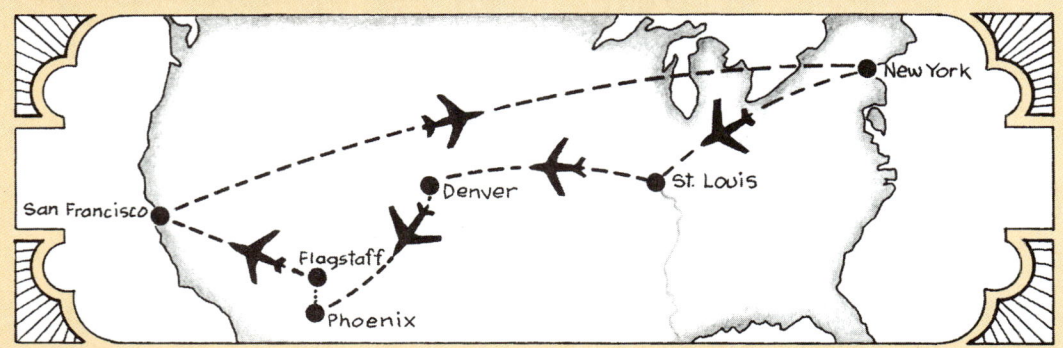

Schedule
Day 1, Tuesday to Day 3, Thursday: Sightseeing in New York. Visit the Statue of Liberty, museums, and other sights. **Day 4, Friday:** Fly to St. Louis and enjoy a tour of the waterfront area, and an evening on a Mississippi riverboat. **Day 5, Saturday:** Denver—Visit museums to see famous exhibits on American Indians; afternoon tour of The Mint. **Day 6, Sunday:** Fly to Phoenix. Go by bus to Flagstaff through Canyon Country. **Day 7, Monday and Day 8, Tuesday:** Two unforgettable days exploring the Grand Canyon. **Day 9, Wednesday:** Fly to San Francisco. **Day 10, Thursday to Day 14, Sunday:** Sightseeing includes a fabulous bay cruise, Golden Gate Park, Chinatown, Alcatraz, Candlestick Park (in baseball season only), and Big Sur. **Day 15, Monday:** Nonstop flight back to New York.

PRICE INCLUDES
Roundtrip airfare • Bus tours and transportation by Tourways Bus Company • Fourteen nights hotel accommodation • Continental breakfasts • Sightseeing tours and land transportation

---

GLOSSARY
cruise—pleasure trip on a boat
ex·**hi**·bit—a special show, usually about one kind of thing
ex·**plore**—go through a place, looking at it carefully
fab·u·lous—very special, very good
in·**clude**—place in the same group of people, ideas, things
tour—a trip for enjoyment
un·for·**get**·table—very hard to forget

---

1. **Read the tour advertisement above. Then write the answers to these questions on your paper.**

   a. How many days is the tour?
   b. What cities does the tour include?
   c. How long does the tour stay at the Grand Canyon?
   d. What interesting things can you see in St. Louis?
   e. How much does the tour cost?
   f. Does the price include hotels? Does it include dinners?

2. **Ask your partner about the trip he/she took last summer on the coast to coast tour. Ask questions like these.**

   a. Where did you begin your trip?
   b. What did you see there?
   c. Where were you on the fourth day?
   d. When did you go to Denver?
   e. How long were you there?

Listening

Copy the chart on your paper. Listen to Sarah Jones talking about a typical day in her life. Take notes and check what Sarah does in the correct column on your chart.

Does Sarah Jones . . .	ALWAYS	OFTEN	USUALLY	HARDLY EVER	NEVER
get up at six	???	???	???	???	???
take a shower?	???	???	???	???	???
drink coffee?					
eat bacon?					
take the train to work?					
take the bus?					
start work at nine?					
work late?					
listen to music?					
listen to jazz?					
listen to rock?					

Practice Points

1. **Copy the following sentences. Use *one* or *the other one* in place of any words you can. The first one is done for you.**

   a. There are two men on the street. The tall man is my father. The short man is my uncle. *There are two men on the street. The tall one is my father. The short one is my uncle.*

   b. There are two women in the yard. The woman on the left is busy. The woman on the right isn't.
   c. Look at these photos. This photo is San Francisco. That photo is Boston.
   d. Take these boxes. Put the big box in the kitchen. Put the little box in the hall.
   e. There are two children in the room. The boy on the left is David. The boy on the right is Chris.
   f. Do you want to have this CD or the CD over there?
   g. Two books are on the table. Read the book on the top first. Read the book on the bottom later.
   h. Look at these drawings. The red drawing is mine. The blue drawing is Judy's.

2. **Copy the paragraphs below and write about a typical day in your life. Use *always*, *often*, *usually*, *hardly ever*, and *never*, and other words to describe your day. Remember to indent the first line of each new paragraph.**

   I *always* get up at *six* o'clock. I . . . take a shower before I get dressed. I . . . have breakfast at . . . o'clock. I . . . have juice, . . . , and . . . . I . . . have . . . ; I hate . . . ! I . . . leave for school at . . . o'clock. I . . . take the bus. My mother . . . drives me. I . . . walk to school.

   I get to school at . . . . First I go to . . . . My teacher's name is . . . . Later I go to . . . . I . . . have lunch at . . . o'clock. After lunch, I go to . . . . My favorite school subject is . . . . I hate . . . .

   After school, I usually . . . . I hardly ever . . . . We eat dinner at . . . , and I . . . after dinner. I . . . go to bed at . . . o'clock. I . . . fall asleep right away.

3. **A verb is a word that describes an action or state of being. Some examples of verbs are: *is, are, go, sleep, hate, have*. Look at the paragraphs that you completed for exercise 2. Write a list of all the verbs in the paragraphs. Then compare your list with your partner's.**

4. **Use the chart that you completed about Sarah's day in the listening exercise on page 11. Write ten questions and answers like these.**

   What time does she get up? She always gets up at six.
   Does she work late? No, she hardly ever works late.

Let's Rock!

Turn to page 125.
Listen to the song *Going on Vacation*.
Read the words as you listen. Then sing along!

Check Points

Communication Points

Make guesses	I think that's Los Angeles. That must be New York.
Agree or disagree	That's right. No, you're wrong.
Locate and identify people	Who are the two boys at the bus stop? The one on the right is Bill. The other one is John.

1.
That must be I think that's	New York. Los Angeles.

2.

That's right.	
No, you're wrong.	That's the Golden Gate Bridge, and it's in San Francisco.

3.

Who are the two men next to the tent?

4.

The one on the	right / left	is	Uncle Jim.
The other one			my dad.

5.

I	always / often / usually / hardly ever / never	get up at seven.

Words and Expressions

bacon	juice	photo	wrong		
before	later	subject		yard	garden—if grass or plants
box	men	uncle			yard—if paved
drawings	must	women	hardly ever		

Read a poem

NOLAN DAVIS

I stepped in front of the fun house mirror
In the local amusement park.
My face contorted,
My body elongated,
My legs distorted,
All parts of me pulled in various directions
By people who say they know what's best for me.
Parents, teachers, friends
Shout advice from every corner of the park,
But all I hear is the same tinny music
Over and over again.
I wonder if I'll ever see
A clear image of myself.

Mel Glenn

3 CAMPING IN THE WEST

JANET: Come on, let's see some more slides.
TIM: Yes, they're terrific.
BILL: This is...yes, this must be on the Arizona, Utah border. Monument Valley.
CAROL: Terrific, isn't it? And look, the whole family is in front of the camper.
JOHN: Whose camper is that? Is it yours?
CAROL: No, it isn't. It's Uncle Jim's.

JANET: Hey, look! There's Bill next to a real cowboy!

CAROL: And that's me, hiding behind a giant sequoia.
JOHN: Look at the size of that tree! Where was it?
CAROL: In the Muir Woods, in California.

JANET: Oh, this is a funny one. Who's that under the tent?
BILL: My cousin Faye. The tent fell in. She didn't think it was very funny then.
JOHN: I bet. But was camping really fun?
CAROL: It was okay.
BILL: It was *great!* I want to go again next year.

Communication Points
Locate people and things

The car is in front of the camper, and the tent is behind the camper. The camper is under a tree. The tree is next to a river. A very large bear is between the river and the picnic table. That's why the family is up in the tree! Until a minute ago, they were sitting around the picnic table.

1. **Read the paragraph above and look at the picture. Then ask and answer questions about the picture with your partner.**

   A: Where's the car?
   B: It's in front of the camper.

2. **Draw a campground on a piece of paper. Put a car, a camper, a tent, a picnic table, a river, and a family anywhere you like. Work with a partner and ask and answer questions about your pictures.**

Identify people's possessions

> It's my camera. It's mine.
> It's your tent. It's yours.
> It's his bicycle. It's his.
> It's her car. It's hers.
> It's our fishing rod. It's ours.
> It's their camper. It's theirs.

1. **Work with a partner. Find out who the things belong to by following the maze.**

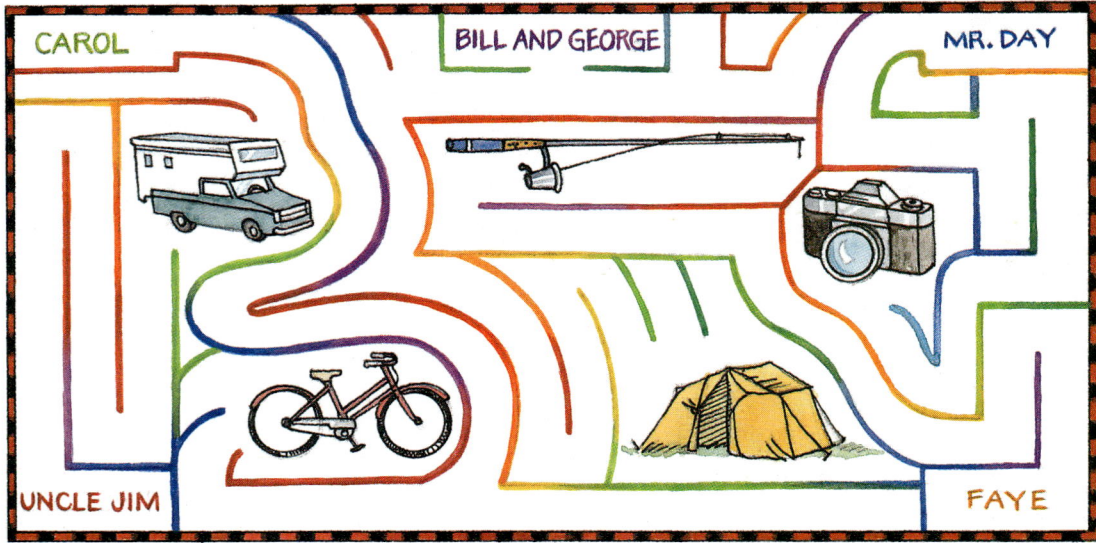

2. **Ask and answer with your partner. Use these words:** *bicycle, camera, camper, fishing rod, tent.*

> A: Whose camper is this?
> B: It's Uncle Jim's.
> A: Are you sure?
> B: Yes, it's his.

3. **Work with a partner. Find out who the clothes belong to by following the maze.**

4. Ask and answer with your partner. Use these words: *boots, gloves, pants, shoes, socks.*

> A: Whose gloves are these?
> B: They're Carol's.
> A: Are you sure?
> B: Yes, they're hers.

5. Now practice with your partner. Use the mazes on page 16.

> A: Faye, are these your socks?
> B: Yes, they're mine.

> A: Bill and George, is this your car?
> B: No, it's not ours. It's Aunt Judy's.

> A: Carol, isn't this your bicycle?
> B: Yes, it is.
> A: I thought it was yours.

Language Points
Problem solving

Solve this problem with your partner. In the front row of a class are five desks occupied by Tran, Paul, Joy, Susan, and Margaret. The boys do not sit next to each other. A girl does not sit next to a girl. Joy has the middle desk and Tran is on her left. Margaret sits next to Paul. Decide where each person sits.

Listening

Listen to the dialogue and complete the following sentences on your paper.

1. John's father, Mr. Cooper, is . . . .
2. The motorcycle is . . . the car.
3. There are a lot of people . . . .
4. John's mother, Mrs. Cooper, is . . . .
5. John is . . . .

Reading about sports
MOTOCROSS: FAST, WILD, AND VERY POPULAR!

What is one of the hottest sporting events these days? You don't have to travel far to discover the answer to that question. It's motocross. There are major motocross tournaments all over the globe: Argentina, France, Brazil, Belgium, Mexico, Japan, and the United States.

Motocross is a physically demanding sport which requires the athlete to ride a motorcycle round and round a dirt track. The racetracks are especially designed to test the rider's skill, physical and mental strength, and stamina. Trained riders often soar 50–70 feet in the air and risk broken bones as they race over hilly tracks in pursuit of championship honors and money prizes.

This is a sport that is most definitely a young person's sport. The average age of riders is 23. Believe it or not, they retire by age 28 in most cases. Some riders join racing teams that are sponsored by motorcycle manufacturers. Professional motocross riders can often earn six-figure incomes by endorsing products. That doesn't even include the winnings they receive for placing in the top ranks of the sport!

A motocross race consists of a series of elimination rounds or "heats." Riders receive points based on the place they finish at the end of each race. The national champ is the rider with the most points in one racing season. Pedro Gonzalez is one of the most famous champs in the sport. He is often called the "fastest man in Mexico." His popularity has helped increase the popularity of motocross.

Superstar riders like Jeremy McGrath and Jeff Stanton ride their motorcycles at competitions before crowds of 40,000 people. Indoor motocross events are called *supercross*. Specially designed tracks are set up in large sports stadiums. The tracks include many tight turns and jumps, unlike motocross tracks which go over open fields and high hills. McGrath says that supercross demands much more riding finesse than outdoor motocross. "I'm more of a technical rider than one who hammerheads it through the turns and jumps," he says. McGrath's riding style has amazed motocross fans from around the world. He recently broke all records by winning ten events in one season!

1. **Read the passage. Do you know what the words below mean? Often you can understand the meaning of a word by the context, or how it is used in a sentence. First scan the passage to find these words. Then match the words with the correct meanings and write them on your paper.**

globe	tournaments	hottest
soar	finesse	endorsing

   a. supporting
   b. the world
   c. most popular
   d. ability to do something difficult in a skillful way
   e. organized competitions in a sport
   f. go or fly up very high

2. **Read each of the sentences below and decide if it is true or false. If it is false, write the true sentence on your paper.**

   a. Supercross racing is easier than motocross racing.
   b. Pedro Gonzalez is a very fast racer from Brazil.
   c. Motocross racing is physically demanding.
   d. Professional motocross racers make a lot of money.
   e. Some motocross racers go over 50 feet in the air.
   f. There are no motocross races in Mexico.
   g. Jeremy McGrath and Jeff Stanton race in front of large crowds.
   h. McGrath broke racing records by winning eight events in one season.

Writing

Write your answers in paragraph form on your paper.

   a. What are some popular sports in your country? Do many people attend these sporting events? Describe why people like the sport.
   b. Who is your favorite sports star? Describe why you like her/him.

Reading advertisements

1. Read the advertisements and write the words that show ownership. For example, *a. yours.*

2. **Copy the sentences on your paper and fill in the blanks with *mine, yours, his, hers, ours,* or *theirs*.**

   a. The pleasure is your pleasure. The pleasure is . . . .
   b. They're your shoes for only $35. They're . . . for only $35.
   c. What about her coat? What about . . . ?
   d. Their burger is only a burger. . . . is only a burger.
   e. But our burger is the burger. But . . . is the burger.
   f. Look at my teeth. Look at . . . .
   g. Their key to success is reading. . . . is reading.

Writing

Work together with your partner and write two advertisements. Draw pictures to go with them.

Practice points

a.

b.

1. **Copy and complete the paragraphs about the pictures. Use these prepositions: *between, behind, on, around, next to, under, in front of*. (Prepositions are words that tell *where*.)**

   a. There is a big race today at North High School. Any student from 13 to 16 years old can run. There is a track . . . the field. Bill is . . . John who is second. Tim is . . . John, and Mike is . . . Tim and Don.

   b. Bill is now . . . the stand and all of his friends are happy for him. . . . the stand you can see his sister Carol . . . Janet. Mrs. Day is . . . Janet and Mr. Day.

2. **Write all the questions and answers used in exercise 2 on page 16.**

   Whose camper is this? It's Uncle Jim's.
   Are you sure? Yes, it's his.

3. A noun is a word that is the name of something. These words are nouns: *book, pen, house, dog, city, park*. They often come after words like a, an, the, two, his, her, etc. For example, an *apple*, the *boy*, his *book*. Look at the paragraph under the picture on page 15. Make a list of all the nouns in the paragraph. Compare your list with your partner's.

Check Points

Communication Points

Locate people and things   The car is in front of the camper.
Identify people's possessions   Whose camper is this? It's Uncle Jim's.

1.
Where's the	bear? tent? family?

2.
It's They're	behind in front of next to under up in	the tree.
	between	the tree and the river.
	around	the picnic table.

3.
Whose	camper bicycle	is this?
	gloves socks	are these?

4.
It's	mine. yours. hers. his.
They're	ours. theirs. Uncle Jim's.

5.
Isn't Is	this your bicycle?

6.
Yes,	it is.
No,	it's not ours.

Words and Expressions

around	between	fishing rod	ours	tent	whose
aunt	boots	gloves	pants	theirs	yours
bear	camper	hers	shoes	under	
behind	cousin	mine	socks	until	

Are you sure?   in front of

Present	Past
think	thought

22 UNIT THREE

Communication Points

Ask and talk about dates

1. **Read these.**

1st—first	11th—eleventh	21st—twenty-first
2nd—second	12th—twelfth	22nd—twenty-second
3rd—third	13th—thirteenth	23rd—twenty-third
4th—fourth	14th—fourteenth	24th—twenty-fourth
5th—fifth	15th—fifteenth	25th—twenty-fifth
6th—sixth	16th—sixteenth	26th—twenty-sixth
7th—seventh	17th—seventeenth	27th—twenty-seventh
8th—eighth	18th—eighteenth	28th—twenty-eighth
9th—ninth	19th—nineteenth	29th—twenty-ninth
10th—tenth	20th—twentieth	30th—thirtieth
		31st—thirty-first

2. **Ask and answer with your partner.**

   > A: What's the date today/tomorrow?
   > B: The second of October.

   > A: What was the date yesterday?
   > B: The . . . of . . . .

3. **Now say these dates to your partner.**

   10/22/39 = The twenty-second of October, nineteen thirty-nine.

1/19/78	3/10/82	6/7/76	7/25/91
4/11/75	4/1/58	8/3/64	3/30/74
5/5/94	9/18/72	10/30/85	11/20/93

Ask and talk about birthdays

1. **Ask and answer questions about birthdays. Use the charts below.**

   > A: Isn't Bill's birthday in October?
   > B: Yes, it's on October the eighth.

BIRTHDAYS	
Bill	October 8th
Carol	March 7th
Tim	August 20th

John	September 15th
Janet	January 1st
Diana	November 3rd
Carlos	May 29th

2. **Ask your classmates about their birthdays.**

   > A: When is your birthday?
   > B: It's on . . . the . . . .

Ask and talk about past and future events

1. Look at the calendar above. Ask and answer questions with your partner.

> A: What was Carol doing on Monday the seventh?
> B: She was skating.
> A: And where were Bill and John on Saturday the twelfth?
> B: They were at the soccer game.

2. Make your own calendar for next week. Ask and answer questions with your partner.

> A: Are you going to play tennis on Monday the . . . ?
> B: Yes, I am./No, I'm going to . . . .

Identify people's clothing

Karen   Judy   Andy   Mrs. Rose   Frank

1. Whose clothes are these? Can you guess?

dress   boots   t-shirt   shirt   purse   shoes   jeans   hat

shorts   tie   sneakers   sweater   gloves   belt   shoes   skirt

blouse   purse   jacket   pants   socks   jacket   sandals   sweatshirt

A: Whose tie is this?	A: Whose purses are these?
B: It's Frank's.	B: They're the girls'.

2. Ask and answer with your partner.

A: Are these shorts Andy's?	A: Is this sweater Judy's?
B: Yes, they're his.	B: Yes, it's hers.

Language Points
Reading for pleasure
ARE YOU ONE OF THESE PEOPLE?

***Enthusiastic**
 but shy*

You are very enthusiastic and get excited and happy about your work. You are always ready to give a hand and help your friends. But you are a little shy and afraid to meet new people. And if things don't go very well you feel unhappy and depressed.

***Self-confident**
 but lose your temper*

You have plenty of confidence in yourself and know that you are smart and can do anything. You always remember things which are important. You are very generous. But you lose your temper very quickly, and get angry at your friends.

***Ambitious**
 but critical*

You are ambitious and have great ideas about what you will do with your life; you want to be an important person. You are always honest and tell the truth. And you are generous and like to give things to your friends. But sometimes you are too critical; your friends do not like to be told what is wrong with them.

***Imaginative**
 but forgetful*

You are very imaginative and are always thinking up new ideas and new ways to do things. But you do not like to take advice and you will not listen to your friends when they tell you what you should do. And you are very forgetful and can't remember to get your work done on time.

***Independent**
 but moody*

You are independent and think for yourself and decide for yourself. But you are very moody and jump from being very happy to being very depressed and sad. And sometimes you are unrealistic about people and do not look at what they are really like.

***Sociable**
 but lazy*

You like success and being able to do the things you want to do. You are sociable and like to be with other people. You are unhappy if you are unsuccessful and can't do something you want to do. But sometimes you are lazy and don't feel like working or doing anything.

> **GLOSSARY**
> am·**bi**·tious—wanting to become famous or get ahead in your work
> **gen**·er·ous—glad to share whatever you have
> i·**mag**·i·na·tive—able to think up ideas which are new or not real
> lose your **tem**·per—become angry
> shy—afraid of meeting new people
> suc·**cess**—getting what you want

1. Match the words below with the phrases on the right. Then write them on your paper.

a. independent
b. lazy
c. enthusiastic
d. critical
e. moody
f. shy

g. a person who is afraid to meet new people
h. a person who tells others what is wrong with them
i. a person who changes from being happy to being depressed
j. a person who thinks and decides for himself or herself
k. a person who doesn't want to work or do anything
l. a person who is happy and excited about his or her work

2. Do any of these descriptions fit you? Why or why not? What are some other words you can use to describe yourself? (You may want to use some of the words from exercise 1.) Discuss these questions with your partner.

Listening

Listen to the radio program *Secrets of the Stars*. Some famous TV personalities are being described. On your paper, write the name of each star and three things about the star's personality.

Practice Points

1. Look at the examples. Then write all the ways dates can be written. Be sure to include commas between the day's date and the year (August 2, 1994).

   We say: the second of August, nineteen ninety-four
   We write: August 2, 1994   August 2nd, 1994   8/2/94

   a. the twenty-second of October, nineteen thirty-nine
   b. the tenth of March, nineteen seventy-one
   c. the nineteenth of January, nineteen fifty-two
   d. the seventh of June, nineteen ninety-three
   e. the fourth of July, seventeen seventy-six
   f. the twenty-fifth of December, nineteen eighty-seven
   g. the twenty-eighth of February, nineteen forty-one
   h. the first of August, nineteen eighty-one
   i. the thirteenth of April, nineteen ninety-five
   j. the fifth of May, nineteen eighty

2. Write three sentences from each pair of words, using the correct pronouns. (Pronouns are words that take the place of nouns or names. For example, *I, you, he, his, her, our, their, mine, yours.*) The first one is done for you.

   a. Jane/hat
      That's Jane's hat. It's hers. Give it to her.
   b. Bill/tie
   c. Jean/T-shirt
   d. Bill and John/book
   e. my/belt
   f. our/football

3. Write three sentences from these pairs of words, using the correct pronouns. The first one is done for you.

   a. Jane/sneakers
      Those are Jane's sneakers. They're hers. Give them to her.
   b. Bill/shorts
   c. my/glasses
   d. Janet and Carol/magazines
   e. our/shoes
   f. Carol/jeans

Check Points

Communication Points

Ask and talk about dates	What's the date today/tomorrow? The second of October.
Ask and talk about birthdays	Isn't Bill's birthday in October? Yes, it's on October the eighth. When is your birthday? It's on March the seventh.
Ask and talk about past and future events	What was Carol doing on Monday the seventh? She was skating. Are you going to play tennis on Monday the seventh? Yes, I am./No, I'm going to the dentist's.
Identify people's clothing	Whose purses are these? They're the girls'.

1. | Isn't | Carol's / Bill's | birthday in | March? / October? |

2. | Yes, it's on | March the seventh. / the twenty-second of October. |

3. | Are you going to play | tennis / soccer | on | Monday / Friday | the | fifth? / ninth? |

4. | Yes, I am.
No, I'm going to the dentist's. |

5. | 10/22/39 |
   | October twenty-second, nineteen thirty-nine |
   | October 22nd, 1939. |
   | The twenty-second of October, nineteen thirty-nine |

6. | Whose | sneakers are these? / tie is this? |

7. | They're the girls'. / It's Frank's. |

8. | Are these shorts Andy's? / Is this belt Judy's? |

9. | Yes, | they're his. / it's hers. |

Words and Expressions

belt	jacket	sandals	skirt	tie	
blouse	jeans	shirt	sneakers	T-shirt	Ordinal numbers 1st to 31st
dress	purses	shorts	sweatshirt		

pants	trousers
rubber boots	wellingtons
sneakers	plimsolls

5 CAN I HELP YOU?

CLERK: Hello! Can I help you?
CAROL: Yes. I'd like a pair of sneakers, please.
CLERK: What size?
CAROL: Umm . . . size ten.
CLERK: For *you?* I think tens would be too big.
CAROL: Oh no, not for me. They're for my brother.
CLERK: I see. The ones over here are very good ones.
CAROL: Uh . . . How much are they?
CLERK: Thirty-eight dollars.
JANET: Gee, Carol. That's pretty expensive.
CAROL: Do you have a cheaper pair? What about those over there?
CLERK: Ah, those. . . . Let me see. Yes, they're twenty-four dollars. But the other ones are better than these.
CAROL: I can't afford the expensive ones. But I think these are too small. Do you have a size ten?
CLERK: Sure. Here you are.
CAROL: What do you think, Janet? Do you think Bill will like them?
JANET: Yeah, I think they're fine.
CAROL: Okay. I'll take these.

Communication Points
Ask and talk about heights

| Vinh | Ellen | Pam | Sam | Maria |
| 6' 8" | 5' 9" | 5' 1" | 6' 3" | 5' 4" |

Ask and answer with your partner.

> A: How tall is Maria?
> B: She's five feet, four inches tall.

Make comparisons

Make sentences comparing people's heights.

> Vinh is taller than Sam. Pam is shorter than Ellen.

CAN I HELP YOU?

Ask and talk about age and height

Ask about Bill and Carol.

> A: How tall was Bill when he was five?
> B: He was three feet six inches tall.
> A: How old is Bill now?
> B: Sixteen.
> A: How much has he grown since he was five?
> B: Two feet two inches.

Make a choice

Use the pictures below to decide what you want to buy. Practice the dialogues with your partner.

A: Hello. Can I help you?
B: Yes, I'd like a . . . , please.

A: Hello. Do you need any help?
B: Yes, I'd like some . . . , please.

Make comparisons

Use the pictures again to compare sizes and prices with your partner.

A: I think these jeans are too big.
B: Here are some smaller ones.

A: Fifteen dollars! I think this hat is too expensive.
B: Here is a cheaper one.

Language Points
Reading about people
NAOMI CAMPBELL: FAME ON THE FASHION PAGES

Who: Naomi Campbell
Height: 5'11"
Hometown: London, England
Career: Fashion model

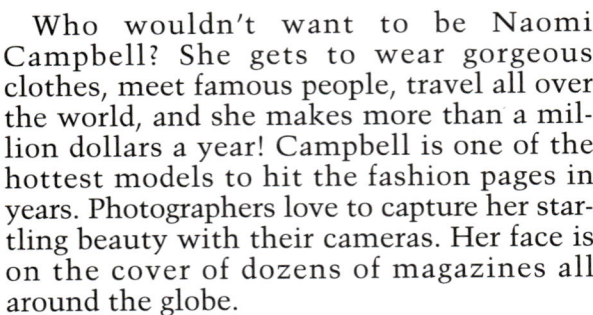

Who wouldn't want to be Naomi Campbell? She gets to wear gorgeous clothes, meet famous people, travel all over the world, and she makes more than a million dollars a year! Campbell is one of the hottest models to hit the fashion pages in years. Photographers love to capture her startling beauty with their cameras. Her face is on the cover of dozens of magazines all around the globe.

London born, Campbell has gotten involved in the recording industry. She has sung on other performers' records and is recording her own songs, too. She enjoys dance music with a strong beat and isn't afraid to face the critics who are ready to discredit her singing ability. The model has also managed to obtain parts in movies and music videos as well as acting jobs on popular U.S. TV shows. Campbell doesn't see any reason why she can't spend her time modeling and singing or doing anything else that she wants to do.

Interestingly enough, Campbell didn't set out to be a model. She wanted to follow her mother's footsteps (literally) and become a contemporary ballet dancer. She attended the London Academy of the Performing Arts and was discovered by a modeling agent at age 15. There was no turning back after that. Naomi began to pose for fashion magazines and started her rise to international fame and success.

Despite all of Campbell's interests, modeling is Campbell's true profession. She says "It's a job." She wears clothes well and moves her body well, a skill that is very important for a model. Campbell has the ability to model without much effort. Francesco Scavullo, an acclaimed photographer, says of Campbell, "If I were a designer, I'd want to create all my clothes for her exclusively. She's so contemporary." That is a high compliment coming from someone like Scavullo who has photographed some of the most noted celebrities in the world.

Campbell has been called the "megamodel of them all" by admiring fashion designers and photographers alike. Campbell's star continues to rise. She has many long-term goals and hopes to incorporate many facets of the fashion and entertainment worlds into her career. There's no doubt whatsoever that she will attain and even surpass her goals.

1. **Do you know these words? Reading the passage will help you understand their meanings. Scan to find the words in the passage. Then write them on your paper next to the correct definition.**

critics	obtain	acclaimed	profession
incorporate	gorgeous	contemporary	startling

   a. career
   b. very attractive
   c. modern
   d. people who say whether a book, movie, or piece of music, etc. is good
   e. surprising
   f. receive
   g. praised
   h. put things together to make a whole

2. **This passage is not written in chronological, or time, order. In other words, it does not start with the beginning of Naomi Campbell's life and go to her present life. Look at these main events in her life and write them in the correct chronological order.**

   a. discovered by a modeling agent
   b. appeared on TV shows
   c. born in London
   d. modeled for fashion magazines
   e. attended the London Academy of the Performing Arts

3. **Now arrange these sentences in correct chronological, or time, order. Write them in paragraph form on your paper. Remember to indent the first line of your paragraph. When you finish you will have a summary of the passage.**

   a. When she was fifteen, she was discovered by a modeling agent.
   b. Then she began receiving parts in movies, videos, and TV shows.
   c. Naomi Campbell was born in London, England.
   d. Naomi became a model and posed for fashion magazines.
   e. She attended the London Academy of the Performing Arts and hoped to become a contemporary ballet dancer.

Writing

What is your favorite kind of magazine? Fashion? Music? Sports? News? Write a short paragraph about the kind of magazines that you like to read.

Listening

Copy the chart on your paper. Listen to the two dialogues and fill in the information on your chart.

WHO IS IT FOR?	WHAT?	HOW BIG?	HOW MUCH?
???	???	???	???

CAN I HELP YOU?

Practice Points

1. **Use the pictures on page 33 and write four dialogues like the example.**

   A: *I think this shirt is too big.*
   B: *Here's a smaller one.*

2. **Copy the sentences and fill in the blanks with *this* or *these*.**

   a. ... sweater is too expensive.
   b. I like ... jeans.
   c. I broke ... glasses last night.
   d. How much is ... hat?
   e. I'd like ... shirt, please.
   f. ... shoes are too small.
   g. Let's buy ... dress.
   h. ... shorts are too big.

3. **Copy the sentences and fill in the blanks with *that* or *those*.**

   a. Do you know ... boy?
   b. ... woman is pretty.
   c. ... slides were great.
   d. Let's go see ... movie.
   e. Give me ... magazines, please.
   f. ... children are noisy.
   g. Look at ... mountains!
   h. I'm going to buy ... hat.

4. **Copy and complete.**

   a. CLERK: Can I help you?
      YOU: ....
      CLERK: What size?
      YOU: ....
      CLERK: Here you are.
      YOU: ....
      CLERK: Twenty-two dollars.

   b. CLERK: These are good tennis shoes. They're thirty-eight dollars.
      YOU: ....
      CLERK: Well, these are cheaper.
      YOU: ....
      CLERK: Eighteen dollars.
      YOU: ....

5. **Write a dialogue about Carol on page 32. Start with *How tall was Carol when she was five?***

Let's Rock!

Turn to page 126.
Listen to the song *Over and Over Again*.
Read the words as you listen. Then sing along!

Check Points

Communication Points

Ask and talk about heights	How tall is Maria? She's five feet, four inches tall.
Make comparisons	Vinh is taller than Sam.
	I think this jacket is too big. Here's a smaller one.
Ask and talk about age and height	How tall was Bill when he was five?
	He was three feet six inches tall.
	How old is Bill now? Sixteen.
	How much has he grown since he was five?
	Two feet two inches.
Make a choice	I'd like a jacket, please.
	I think this jacket is too big.

1.
How tall	is	Maria?	
	was	Bill	when he was five?

2.
She	's	five feet, four	inches tall.
He	was	three feet, six	

3.
How much has he grown since he was	five?
	eight?

4.
Vinh	is	taller	than	Sam.
Tom		shorter		Ellen.

5.
Can I help you?
Do you need any help?

6.
Yes, I'd like	a	jacket,	please.
	some	sneakers,	

7.
This jacket	is	too	big.
These sneakers	are		expensive.

8.
Here's	a	smaller one.
Here are	some	cheaper ones.

Words and Expressions

height   much   size   than
inch   since   slides

Present	Past	have/has +
grow	grew	grown

Read a poem

IN THE SUN

Sit
on your doorstep
or any place.

Sit
in the sun
and lift your face.

Close your eyes and
sun dream.
Soon the warm warm sun
will seem
to fill you up
and
spill over.

Lilian Moore

6 GOING TO A CONCERT

CARLOS: Hurry up—it's late!
SUE: It is? Let's take the bus.
CARLOS: Okay, but the bus is slower than the subway.
SUE: Maybe so, but it's more interesting. And I like looking out the window.
BARBARA: Well, of course, I always like going by cab!
CARLOS: That's the most expensive way of all! We're late, so let's just go by subway.
SUE: Okay, let's go. What line should we take?
BARBARA: Well, the concert is on 33rd Street at 7th Avenue. So we can take the Broadway-7th Avenue line.
CARLOS: Yeah, we can get off at 34th . . .
SUE: Okay, let's *go!*

Communication Points
Express preferences
Make comparisons
Agree or disagree

1. Learn these words.

safe	safer	good	better	dangerous	more dangerous
cheap	cheaper	bad	worse	expensive	more expensive
slow	slower			boring	more boring
fast	faster			exciting	more exciting
nice	nicer			interesting	more interesting
quiet	quieter			comfortable	more comfortable
cold	colder				

2. Make a chart like the one below. Fill in the information about yourself using the words above.

Which do you like more, . . . ?	YOU	WHY?	PARTNER	WHY?
going by subway or bus			???	???
living in a small town or a big city				
playing basketball or football				
watching TV or going to the movies				
listening to rock music or dancing				

3. Now interview your partner and fill in the rest of your chart.

> A: Which do you like more, going by subway or bus?
> B: I like going by bus.
> A: Why?
> B: Because it's more comfortable.

4. Look at your chart from exercise 3. Practice the dialogues with your partner.

> A: I like going by subway because it's cheaper than the bus.
> B: So do I.
>   or
>   I don't. I like going by bus. It's safer.

> A: I love playing basketball because it's faster than football.
> B: Yes, but playing football is more exciting.

5. Make a list of things to compare. Then practice the dialogue with your partner.

reading mysteries or science fiction
studying math or English

> A: Which do you like more—reading mysteries or science fiction?
> B: I like reading mysteries.
> A: Why?
> B: Because . . . .

Language Points
Reading about history
MISS LIBERTY

Wooden forms for part of the left arm. Bartholdi is second from the right.

The statue in France. Later it was taken apart and shipped to America.

The Statue of Liberty is perhaps the best known symbol of the United States. She stands on a small island in New York Harbor, holding her lighted torch up high. New Americans, immigrants from other countries seeking a new way of life, have always found hope in the sight of the statue.

The idea of such a monument was born over a hundred years ago in France. Edouard Laboulaye wanted France to present a gift to the United States that would be a symbol of the ideals of liberty and equality. A young French artist, Frederic Bartholdi, inspired by the pyramids and huge statues in Egypt, designed the mammoth Statue of Liberty. She would be a robed woman with broken chains around her feet. Her right arm would hold a lighted torch; her left arm would hold a book marked with the date of Independence Day, July 4, 1776.

They worked on the statue in Paris from 1875 to 1881. They made a plaster model in sections. They constructed great wooden forms to fit the plaster casts and a thin copper skin to go over the forms. An engineer, Gustave Eiffel, who would later create the Eiffel Tower in Paris, designed the inside steel supports. After the statue was complete it was taken apart and shipped to the United States.

The French had paid the costs of the statue by many small donations. The Americans had agreed to pay the cost of the huge foundation, but the money was hard to collect. Then Joseph Pulitzer, a Hungarian immigrant, took charge. He had become a great newspaper publisher. He began a fund drive to collect money for the base of the statue. He put in the newspaper more than 100,000 names and messages that came with the gifts. Even children gave their pennies. "We send you $1, the money we saved to go to the circus with," wrote one child. The statue was finally unveiled on October 28, 1886.

1. **Copy the sentences and fill in the blanks with the words in the box. Use one for each blank.**

   | liberty   collect   construct   create   symbol   immigrant   descendant |

   a. They have come here from another country to live. They are . . . .
   b. Her grandfather was an immigrant. She is proud to be his . . . .
   c. The Statue of Liberty is a . . . of America.
   d. To design something new is to . . . it.
   e. It was very difficult to . . . enough money for the statue's foundation.
   f. If you are free to do what you want, you have . . . .
   g. Builders . . . bridges, buildings, and roads.

2. **Write the answers to these questions on your paper.**

   a. Where is the Statue of Liberty?
   b. What country gave the statue to the United States?
   c. What ideals does the statue stand for?
   d. What is the date of the United States Independence Day?
   e. Who designed the Eiffel Tower?
   f. When was the statue unveiled?

Writing

Write the answers to these questions on your paper. Then discuss them with your partner.

a. Why do you think Laboulaye wanted France to give the United States a gift?
b. What do you think the lighted torch symbolizes? The broken chains at her feet?
c. The statue was completed in France in 1881, but it wasn't unveiled in the United States until 1886. Why did it take so long?
d. Do you have some symbolic statues in your country? Tell about the statues and what they symbolize.

Reading a subway map

Use the map to answer these questions. Write your answers on a separate piece of paper.

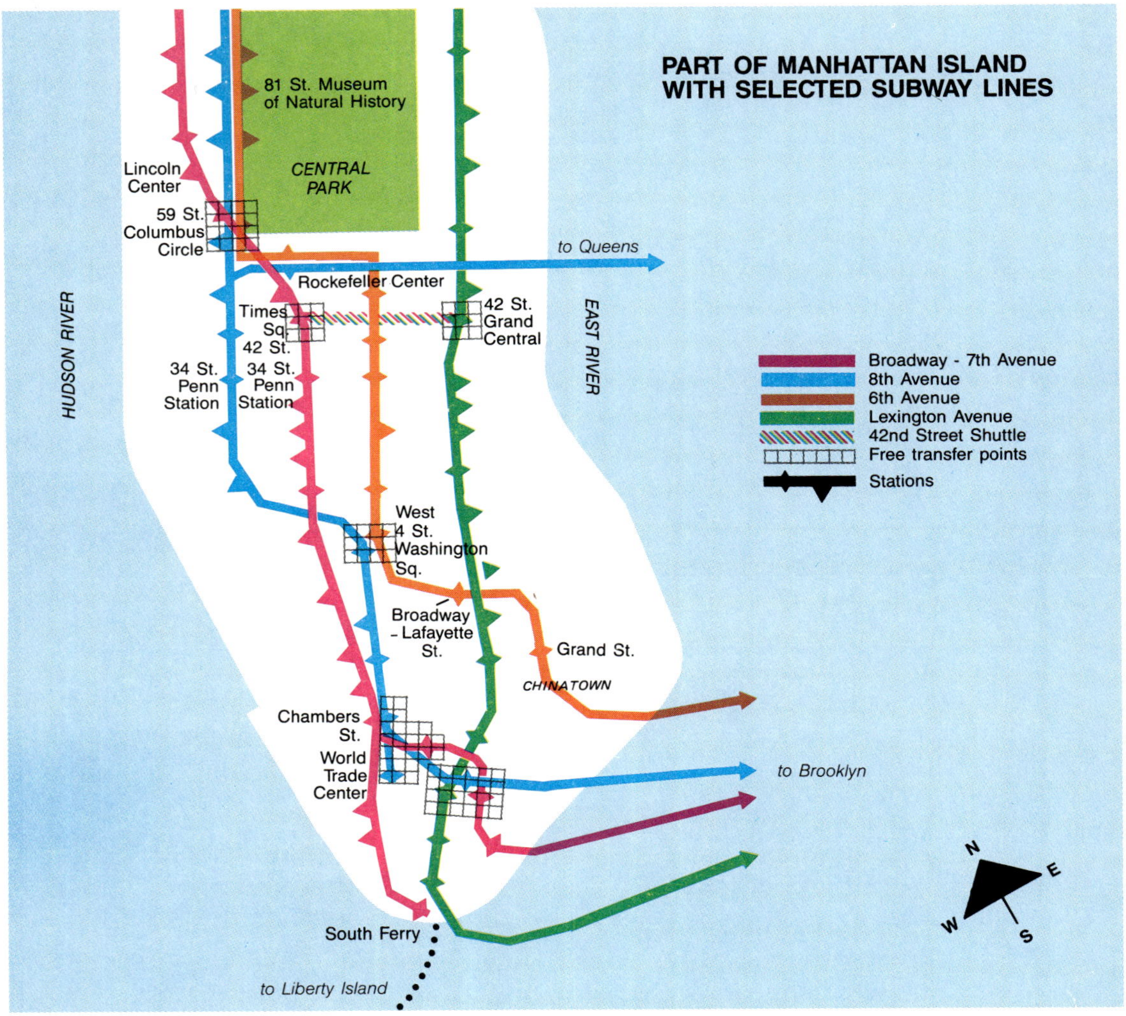

[Map: PART OF MANHATTAN ISLAND WITH SELECTED SUBWAY LINES — showing subway lines: Broadway - 7th Avenue, 8th Avenue, 6th Avenue, Lexington Avenue, 42nd Street Shuttle, Free transfer points, Stations. Landmarks shown include 81 St. Museum of Natural History, Central Park, Lincoln Center, 59 St. Columbus Circle, Rockefeller Center, Times Sq., 42 St., 42 St. Grand Central, 34 St. Penn Station, West 4 St. Washington Sq., Broadway-Lafayette St., Grand St., Chinatown, Chambers St., World Trade Center, South Ferry. Arrows point to Queens, to Brooklyn, to Liberty Island. Labels: Hudson River, East River.]

1. Which subway lines stop at the Museum of Natural History?
2. Which subway line would you take to go from Times Square to Grand Central?
3. Which subway line has a station at the World Trade Center?
4. You want to get from Penn Station to Grand Central. Which subway lines will you take? At what free transfer point will you change lines?
5. You want to go from the Museum of Natural History to Lincoln Center by subway. Tell how you will get there.
6. You want to get from Lincoln Center to Rockefeller Center by subway. Tell how you will get there.

Listening

Listen to the police officer giving directions for the subway. Trace the directions with your finger on the map, starting at Lincoln Center. Where are Carlos, Barbara, and Bill going?

42 UNIT SIX

Guessing game

Look at the map on page 42. Decide to go somewhere on the map. Tell your partner *only* your starting point. Your partner will try to guess your destination by asking questions like these.

Did you take the 8th Avenue line?
Did you go north or south?
Did you change lines?
Did you get off at Washington Square?

Practice Points

1. Adjectives are words that describe nouns or people. For example, These shoes are too *small*. It's an *expensive* car. Frank is *taller* than Sarah is. Below is a list of adjectives. Write the adjectives and their opposites, choosing from these words: *old, bad, small, early, expensive, dangerous, fast, hot, short, noisy, little.*

   a. cheap   d. quiet   g. late
   b. slow   e. cold   h. tall
   c. safe   f. big   i. good

2. Write ten sentences making comparisons. Use the correct forms of the adjectives (*a.–i.*) in the list above.

   This dress is cheaper than that one.

3. Make comparisons using *more . . . than* and the adjectives in parentheses.

   a. Rolls-Royce/Volkswagen (expensive)

   A Rolls-Royce is more expensive than a Volkswagen.

   b. gold/silver (valuable)
   c. Cadillac/Toyota (expensive)
   d. movies/TV (interesting)
   e. Chinese/English (difficult)
   f. apples/melons (delicious)
   g. countryside/city (beautiful)
   h. armchair/desk chair (comfortable)
   i. traveling by car/walking (dangerous)
   j. going to a party/staying at home (exciting)

4. Complete these sentences on your paper. The first one is done for you.

   a. In my town, meat (cheap/expensive) fish.

   In my town, meat is cheaper than fish.

   b. A motorcycle (fast/slow) a bicycle.
   c. Traveling by bicycle (safe/dangerous) traveling by car.
   d. I am (tall/short) my partner.
   e. I am (old/young) my partner.
   f. New York (big/small) Boston.
   g. Montreal (warm/cold) Rio de Janeiro.
   h. A train (slow/fast) a plane.
   i. Rock music (boring/exciting) jazz.

5. Read the chart below. Then complete the sentences on your paper.

| I | prefer
like
love
hate | traveling by plane. |

a. Barbara prefers . . . (travel by plane).
b. Carlos likes . . . (travel by subway).
c. Ann hates . . . (live in the city).
d. Mike and Tom love . . . (go to the movies).
e. I . . . (wash dishes).
f. I . . . (play baseball).
g. I . . . (dance to rock music).
h. I . . . (eat ice cream).

Check Points

Communication Points

Express preferences/
Make comparisons

Which do you like more, going by subway or bus?
I like going by bus. Why? Because it's more comfortable.

Agree or disagree

I like going by subway because it's cheaper than the bus. So do I./I don't. I like going by bus. It's safer./
Yes, but going by bus is safer.

1.

| Which do you like more, | going by subway or bus? |
| | playing basketball or football? |

2.

I	like love	going by	bus	because it's	more comfortable.		
			subway		cheaper	than	the bus.
		playing	basketball		faster		football.

3.

So do I.	
I don't. I like going by	subway.
	bus.
Yes, but playing football	is more exciting.

Words and Expressions

better	dangerous	gold	nice	silver
boring	delicious	interesting	quiet	valuable
countryside	exciting	more	safe	worse

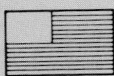

subway
passage under road
truck

tube or underground
subway
lorry

Communication Points

Express opinions

great	the greatest	exciting	the most exciting
funny	the funniest	handsome	the most handsome
loud	the loudest	beautiful	the most beautiful
wild	the wildest	fabulous	the most fabulous
cool	the coolest	incredible	the most incredible
fine	the finest	brilliant	the most brilliant
good	the best	romantic	the most romantic

1. **Make a list of your favorite movie stars, TV stars, singers, bands, dancers, etc. Then make sentences about them using the words above.**

   <u>Movie Stars</u>   <u>TV Stars</u>   <u>Singers</u>
   Tom Cruise   Patrick Stewart   Whitney Houston
   Julia Roberts

   Mel Gibson is handsome. But Tom Cruise is the most handsome movie star.

2. **Ask and answer with your partner.**

   A: Who's your favorite movie star?
   B: ....
   A: Really? Why?
   B: Because ... is the ....

3. **Ask and answer with your partner.**

   A: Do you think Tom Cruise is as handsome as Mel Gibson?
   B: Oh, sure. I think Tom Cruise is more handsome than Mel Gibson.

   A: Do you think Julia Roberts is as good as Demi Moore?
   B: No, I think Demi Moore is better than Julia Roberts.

SPINNER MUSIC
COLLECTOR'S CHOICE SALE!

Add these great CDs to your collection and save!
This week only—20% off our already <u>low low</u> prices!

TOP FORTY HITS OF THIS YEAR!
Two fabulous CDs with the best, most exciting, and best loved hits! Great for dancing.

NEW WAVE HITS
The latest hits from the 747s, the New Yorkers, Queenie and the Coffee Pots and five more favorite groups. Hottest new wave hits!

BEETHOVEN'S PIANO CONCERTOS
Beethoven's five great piano concertos played by one of Germany's most gifted players. The world's most beautiful piano music!

RAVER RAPS
Fantastic new recording by rap's newest and biggest star! #1 for 35 weeks! Includes "Down the Street," "Go Back, Go Forward," and "Hit the Wall Again."

MICHAEL BOLTON
All of this soulful singer's greatest (and most romantic) hits are included in this collection: "Soul Provider," "Sittin' on the Dock of the Bay," "When a Man Loves a Woman," and more.

All at the home of <u>Low</u>, <u>Low</u> prices—
SPINNER RECORDS

At the Hillside Mall
Bellview
Intersection of
Rt. 29 and Rt. 6

Hours:
Monday–Saturday
10A.M.–9P.M.
Sunday
12:00P.M.–6:00P.M.

4. Look at the advertisement and choose the CD you like best. Then work in groups of four and talk to your partners.

> A: Which CD did you choose?
> B: *The Top Forty Hits of This Year.*
> A: Why?
> B: Because it's the most exciting dance music.

THE BEST SINGER

Language Points
Reading about people
AGING ROCKERS: BETTER THAN EVER!

Tina Turner

Is there rock after 40? How about 50? You bet! The list of aging rock stars is a who's who of music. The Rolling Stones, Paul McCartney, Tina Turner, Neil Young, Bob Dylan, Aretha Franklin . . . Do you need more proof that oldies are goodies? Aerosmith, Van Morrison, Bonnie Raitt, Grateful Dead, Rod Stewart, etc. etc. etc.

It is nearly inconceivable that the rock stars of yesteryear—from the Stone Age 1960s and 1970s—are still alive and kicking and rockin' and rollin' just as hard as they did way back then. Paul McCartney, who first came to international fame in the early 1960s says "When I first started out in the business I never imagined that I would still be doing it now." McCartney is still recording, doing concert dates, and making more than $1 million a night.

Likewise, Mick Jagger once said "I'd rather be dead than sing 'Satisfaction' when I'm 45." Since he's a good deal older than that now, he obviously changed his mind. He's still recording with the Rolling Stones and has even done a solo album which received good reviews.

Tina Turner is a grandmother. Yet, she continues to tour and tour and tour. She is perhaps the most highly recognizable female rock star in the world. She says "I can sing and dance better than I can do anything else. . . I never did drugs, drank alcohol. I never abused myself. . . But people don't expect rock-and-roll people to care about themselves."

Other rockers like Rod Stewart, Eric Clapton, and Bonnie Raitt have not been so fortunate. Their years of drug and alcohol abuse took their toll and it was a long, hard road to travel to get back on top. They have cleaned up their personal lives and their musical careers are back on track.

Rock has, indeed, grown up. It has become mainstream, an acceptable (in most cases) form of entertainment and popular culture. Ray Davies, of the Kinks, says "Parents have always come to our gigs. In the beginning it was to make sure their kids got home. Now they're bringing their own kids to witness something they enjoyed when they were young."

Could it be that parents and teenagers now have something in common? Do they enjoy a lot of the same music? It's an interesting concept!

Paul McCartney

1. Do you know these words? Reading the passage will help you understand their meanings. Scan to find the words in the passage. Then write them on your paper next to the correct definition.

   | abused | fortunate | gig | aging |
   | recognizable | obviously | inconceivable | solo |

   a. not to be believed
   b. lucky
   c. to know the name of someone
   d. alone
   e. used wrongly
   f. growing older
   g. easy to see
   h. show

2. True or False? Write the sentences and true or false on your paper.

   a. Paul McCartney became famous in the 1970s.
   b. Rod Stewart is a young rock singer.
   c. Tina Turner took good care of herself.
   d. Mick Jagger decided to continue his career in rock music after age 45.
   e. Many parents go to rock concerts with their children.
   f. Drugs and alcohol nearly ruined many rock stars' careers.

3. Look at the list of adjectives in exercise 1 on page 46. Write down five or six adjectives you could use to describe some of the rock stars in this article. What adjectives would you *not* use to describe them? Why? Then compare your answers with your partner.

Listening

1. Listen to the telephone call. Write on your paper the date and time of the concert, how many tickets are bought, how much the tickets cost, and the ticket seat numbers.

2. Answer these questions on your paper.

   a. Why did the person have to wait to speak to the ticket clerk?
   b. What kind of concert do you think it is? Why?
   c. Do you think that this is a popular group? Why?
   d. Are these kinds of tickets cheaper or more expensive in your country?

Reading tickets and advertisements

1. Look at the tickets. Decide which one you want and find out the following information.

   a. day of performance/game
   b. time of performance/game
   c. row letter
   d. seat number
   e. price of the ticket
   f. performers/players

THE BEST SINGER 49

2. **Imagine you went to the performance you chose in exercise 1.
Ask and answer questions with your partner about what you saw.**

   a. What day was the performance/game?
   b. What time did it begin?
   c. What was your row number?
   d. What was your seat number?
   e. How much did you pay?
   f. Who did you see?
   g. How was the show/game? Did you like it?

   > A: What day was the performance/game?
   > B: It was on . . . .

3. **Read the advertisement below and complete the paragraph on your paper.**

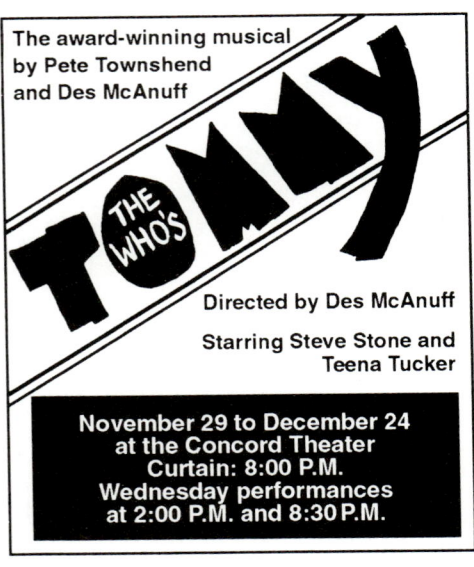

Beginning on . . . 29th, at the . . . Theater, Des . . . directs . . . . This hit musical is by . . . . The stars are . . . and . . . On . . . , there are two performances—at . . . and at 8:00. A matinee is also on . . . at . . . .

Writing

Read the advertisement below and write a paragraph like the one above.

Practice Points

1. Look at these examples using *and, but, so,* and *in fact.*

   a. They ate dinner and went to the store. (sequence)
   b. Deborah is a good singer, but Julie is the best. (contrast)
   c. They were hungry, so they went to a restaurant. (cause/result)
   d. Our team won lots of games this season. In fact, we won four games in November. (details)

2. Read these sentences about the passage on page 48. Write the pairs of sentences on your paper using *and, but, so,* or *in fact.* Use commas as shown in the examples in exercise 1. The first one is done for you.

   a. Mick Jagger said he didn't want to be a rock star after he was 45 years old.
      He changed his mind.

Mick Jagger said he didn't want to be a rock star after he was 45 years old, but he changed his mind.

   b. Tina Turner has sung rock music for many years.
      She's a grandmother!
   c. Eric Clapton had a drug and alcohol problem.
      He cleaned up his personal life.
   d. Parents often go to rock concerts.
      They bring their children with them.
   e. Older rock stars are still very popular.
      Teenagers will probably always like new and different kinds of popular music.

3. Rewrite these sentences on your paper. The first one is done for you.

   a. The Grand Hotel is the (expensive) hotel in Chicago.

The Grand Hotel is the most expensive hotel in Chicago.

   b. New York and London are the (good) places to go to the theater.
   c. Broadway is the (long) avenue in New York City.
   d. The Twin Towers are the (high) skyscrapers in New York.
   e. Greenland is the (large) island in the world.
   f. Rio de Janeiro is the (exciting) city in Brazil.
   g. The (interesting) job of all is being a pilot.

4. **Look at the chart below and write ten sentences using the correct forms of adjectives:** *fast, slow, economical, comfortable, quiet, noisy, safe, expensive, cheap.*

The Venture is faster than the Varm 20KX.
The Varm 20KX is the most economical.

MOTORCYCLES	VENTURE	VARM 20KX	TURBO 95
SPEED	70 mph	55 mph	78 mph
ECONOMY (miles per gallon)	50	56	47
COMFORT ☆ ☆ ☆ very comfortable	☆ ☆ ☆	☆ ☆	☆
NOISE ☆ ☆ ☆ very quiet ☆ very noisy	☆ ☆	☆	☆ ☆ ☆
SAFETY ☆ ☆ ☆ very safe	☆	☆ ☆	☆ ☆ ☆
PRICE	$3,450	$3,300	$4,775

Check Points

Communication Points

Express opinions

Who's your favorite movie star? Tom Cruise.
Why? Because he's the most handsome.

1.
Julie Stewart Her music Her band	is	more	great better. romantic. beautiful.	
		the	greatest best most charming	on this continent.

2.
Do you think	Tom Cruise	is as	handsome	as	Mel Gibson?
	Julia Roberts		good		Demi Moore?

3. Which CD did you choose?

4. The Top Forty Hits of This Year.
Beethoven's Piano Concertos.

5. Why? 6. Because it's the most exciting dance music.
beautiful piano music.

7.

They ate dinner	and	went to the store.
Deborah is a good singer,	but	Julie is the best.
They were hungry,	so	they went to a restaurant.
Our team won lots of games this season.	In fact,	we won four games in November.

Words and Expressions

best	funny	job	skyscrapers	**Present**	**Past**
brilliant	handsome	language	wild	win	won
choose	games	loud	win		
cool	incredible	most			
fabulous	island	nightlife	Really?		

Read a poem

CRYSTAL ROWE
(Track Star)

Allthegirlsarebunched
togetheratthestarting
_____line_____

But

When the gun goes off

I

J

U

M

P

out ahead and
never look back
and
HIT
the

__T__A__P__E

a
WINNER!

Mel Glenn

8 Breakfast Is Ready!

Miss Bennett is Tim's aunt. She has a boarding house for young students in Greenwich Village.

MISS BENNETT: Tim! Paulo! Breakfast is ready!
PAULO: Good morning, Miss Bennett.
MISS BENNETT: Good morning, Paulo.
TIM: Morning, Aunt Mary.
MISS BENNETT: Good morning, dear. Would you like some orange juice?
TIM: I'd love some.
MISS BENNETT: Paulo?
PAULO: No, thank you. I would like some coffee, though. I'll help myself.
TIM: I'd like some rice flakes, please.
MISS BENNETT: Oh, sorry. There isn't any cereal. What about some bacon and eggs instead?
TIM: Okay. How about you, Paulo?
PAULO: Sure. I like bacon and eggs more than anything!
TIM: I'll make the tea, Aunt Mary. Is there any milk?
MISS BENNETT: Yes, there's some in the fridge.

Later

PAULO: Thanks for the breakfast. I have to eat and run, Miss Bennett. I'm late.
MISS BENNETT: Have a good day.
TIM: Bye, Paulo. Here, Aunt Mary, let me help you with the dishes.

Communication Points
Offer and accept or refuse food

Play the role of the waiter. Your partner will order breakfast from the menu above. Change roles.

- A: Good morning. Would you like some juice to start with?
- B: Yes, please, I'd like some . . . juice. /
  No, thanks. No juice for me.
- A: Would you like some cereal?
- B: Yes, I'd like some . . . . /
  No, thanks.
- A: Pancakes? French toast?
- B: Yes, I'll have some . . . with . . . . /
  No, thank you.
- A: What about some eggs this morning?
- B: Yes, please. I'll have two eggs with . . . . /
  No, thanks. No eggs this morning.
- A: (How would you like your eggs?)
- B: (. . . , please.)
- A: Okay. Anything to drink? Coffee, tea, hot chocolate?
- B: Some . . . , please. /
  No, thanks, nothing for me.
- A: Anything else?
- B: Yes, I'd like . . . . /
  No, nothing right now.
- A: Very good. Thank you.

BREAKFAST IS READY!

Express preferences

1. Make a list of your most favorite things to eat for breakfast, lunch, dinner, snack, and dessert. Then practice the dialogue with your partner.

   > A: What do you like best for . . . ?
   > B: I like . . . more than anything!
   > A: Do you like . . . more than . . . ?
   > B: Of course! . . . is my number one favorite.

2. There are five main food groups: meat, fish, and poultry; vegetables; bread; fruit; dairy products. Copy the chart below. Work with your partner to fill in as many foods as you can. Then circle your most favorite foods on your chart.

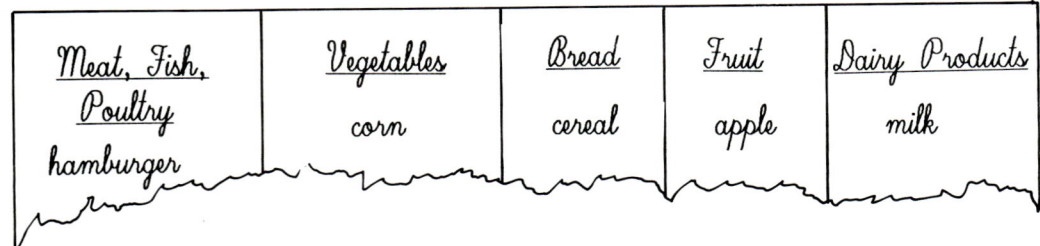

Meat, Fish, Poultry	Vegetables	Bread	Fruit	Dairy Products
hamburger	corn	cereal	apple	milk

Agree or disagree

1. Use the chart you completed above. Practice the dialogue with your partner.

   > A: What is your favorite . . . in the whole world?
   > B: . . . .
   > A: That's my favorite, too. . . . is the best!
   >   *or*
   > That's not my favorite. I like . . . even more than . . . .

2. What would you eat if you could eat only ten things for the rest of your life? Remember, for a healthy body you should eat foods from each of the five main groups. Make a list. Then talk about your list with your partner.

Language Points

Listening

Carol and Bill are making tacos. Listen and find out how much they are going to use of each of the things they need. Copy the card and write the amounts on your paper.

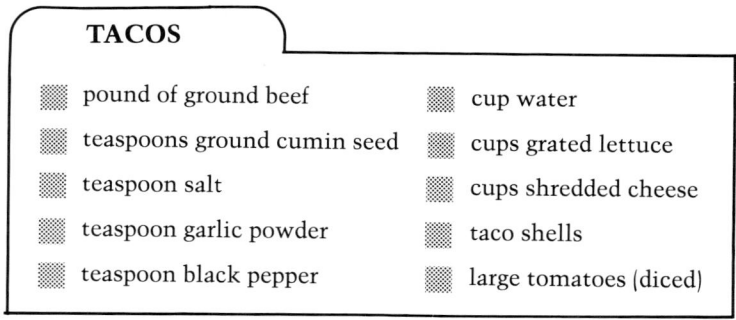

TACOS

- ▨ pound of ground beef
- ▨ teaspoons ground cumin seed
- ▨ teaspoon salt
- ▨ teaspoon garlic powder
- ▨ teaspoon black pepper
- ▨ cup water
- ▨ cups grated lettuce
- ▨ cups shredded cheese
- ▨ taco shells
- ▨ large tomatoes (diced)

Reading a recipe

TACOS RECIPE

Read the recipe instructions. Then look at the pictures. Both the instructions and pictures are in the wrong order. Match the pictures with the instructions and put them in the correct order. On your paper, write the correct instruction beside the letter of the picture in the correct order.

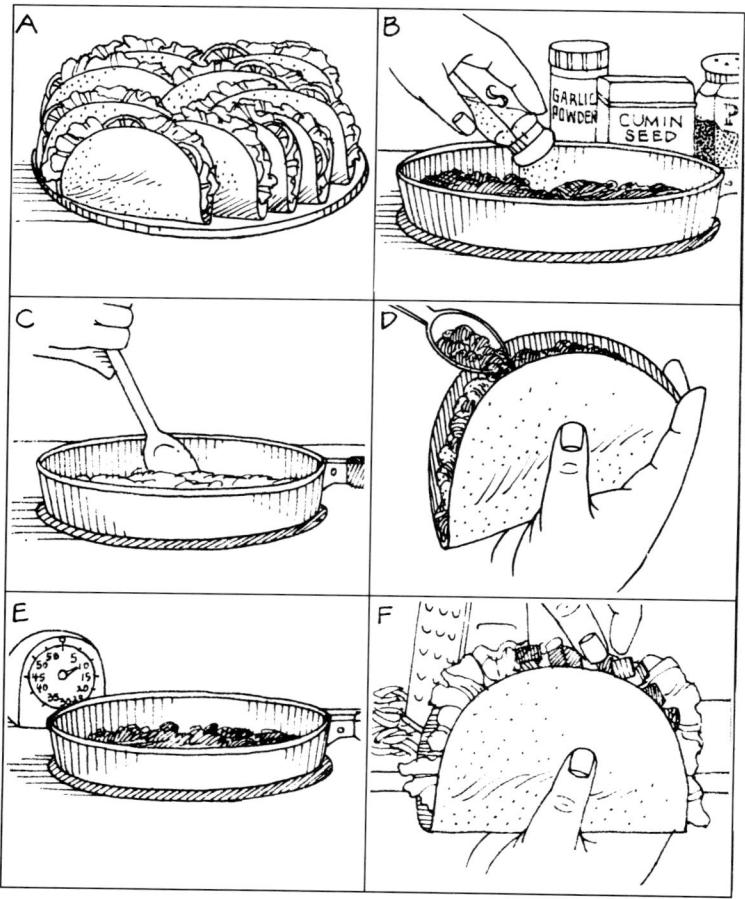

Instructions

- Add seasonings (cumin, salt, pepper, garlic powder) and water to meat. Bring to a boil.
- Lightly brown ground beef in a frying pan.
- Fill taco shells with ground beef.
- Makes 10-12 tacos.
- Add lettuce, tomatoes, and cheese to taco shells.
- Simmer uncovered for 10 minutes.

Reading about culture
AMERICAN FOOD—WHAT IS IT?

A Chinese meal

Mexican Fast Food

New England seafood

Many people think that the most typical American meal is the following: a big, tender steak, a hot baked potato, a fresh green salad, rolls and butter. For dessert, apple pie with ice cream, and coffee.

Americans *do* eat the meal described above, and they eat it often. But it's really not possible to describe one meal as typically American.

Like its people, American food comes from around the world, too. Almost every town across the country has a Chinese restaurant. Americans love egg rolls, noodles, and chop suey. You can also buy many Chinese foods in the supermarket. Millions of Americans are crazy about Mexican food too—tacos, burritos, and enchiladas. Mexican food has even entered the fast food market.

Each fast food restaurant has a specialty. Some of them serve mainly hamburgers and french fries. Another very popular fast food is fried chicken served with coleslaw and biscuits. Along the New England coast all kinds of seafood are offered at little stands. Most of the food is deep-fried. You can get clams, shrimp, or fish.

Maybe Italian food is the foreign food that has become most typical in America. Spaghetti, noodles, macaroni, and pizza are all eaten everywhere in the United States.

Whenever immigrants enter the United States they bring their foods with them. In New York City you can choose from more than 300 restaurants including Japanese, Thai, Vietnamese, Hungarian, Cuban, French, Korean, Spanish, Brazilian, Portuguese, Russian, Swiss—even Mongolian!

GLOSSARY
coast—where the land meets the sea
stuff—things
cra·zy about—extremely fond of
pos·si·ble—it can be done

Read the passage. Then write the answers to these questions on your paper.

a. Which sentence best describes the main idea of the passage?
   1. Americans like international food, such as Chinese, Mexican, and Italian.
   2. It's hard to define the typical American meal because Americans eat so many different kinds of international foods.
   3. The U.S. has a population of people from all over the world.
b. What do many people think is the typical American meal, according to this article?
c. Why is it hard to say what the typical American meal is?
d. What are some international foods that are popular in the U.S.?
e. What kinds of food can you find in American fast food restaurants?

Writing

Choose one of the following and write about it on your paper.

a. Write a paragraph describing the "typical" food of your native country.
b. Write a paragraph describing your favorite meal. Tell why it's your favorite.
c. What's the one thing you know how to cook the best? Write a recipe that tells how you make it.
d. What are some popular international foods in your country? Which do you like the best?

Open dialogue

You are a waitress or waiter in a restaurant. Talk to the customer and take the order.

YOU: ....
CUSTOMER: Good morning.
YOU: ....
CUSTOMER: Yes, please. I'd like some grapefruit juice.
YOU: ....
CUSTOMER: Yes. Corn flakes, please.
YOU: ....
CUSTOMER: Eggs? Yes, please.
YOU: ....
CUSTOMER: Scrambled, please. And I'd like some toast, too.
YOU: ....
CUSTOMER: No, nothing right now.

Practice Points

1. In your own words, write the recipe for tacos. There are six steps. Use the words below.

salt	garlic powder	water	seasonings
lightly brown	ground beef	boil	fill
taco shells	black pepper	tomatoes	meat
simmer	shredded cheese	drain	uncovered
ground cumin seed	grated lettuce	add	diced

2. Write out the open dialogue on page 59.

3. Match the questions and answers and write them on your paper. Then write where you think each conversation takes place: *in a restaurant, in a department store, at home, at the post office, in a shoe store.* The first one is done for you.

   a. Good morning, sir. Would you like some juice to start with?

   h. Yes, please. I'd like some grapefruit juice, please.

   In a restaurant.

   a. Good morning, sir. Would you like some juice to start with?
   b. Can I try on these jeans, please?
   c. How would you like your eggs, ma'am?
   d. Can I have two 40-cent stamps, please?
   e. Do you have these shoes in red?

   f. Here you are. That's 80 cents.
   g. Scrambled.
   h. Yes, please. I'd like some grapefruit juice, please.
   i. Sure. You can try them on in the dressing rooms behind you.
   j. Yes, ma'am. What size?

4. Copy the questions and answer them on your paper using these adverbs: *always, usually, sometimes, hardly ever,* or *never.* Words which are used to tell when or how often are called adverbs.

   Do you have coffee for breakfast?

   No, I never do.

   a. Do you have coffee for breakfast?
   b. Do you eat scrambled eggs for breakfast?
   c. Do you have a sandwich for lunch?
   d. Do you drink milk every day?
   e. Do you eat French toast for breakfast?
   f. Do you drink juice in the morning?

Let's Rock!

Turn to page 127.
Listen to the song *Street Beat*.
Read the words as you listen. Then sing along!

Check Points

Communication Points

Offer and accept or refuse food   Would you like some juice?
         Yes, please. I'd like some orange juice.
         No, thanks. No juice for me.

Express preferences   I like . . . more than anything!
Agree or disagree   That's my favorite, too. . . . is the best!
         That's not my favorite. I like . . . even more than. . . .

1.
Would you like	some juice?
What about	pancakes?
Anything	to drink?
	else?

2.
Yes, please.	I'd like some	orange juice.
		pancakes.
No, thanks.	No juice for me.	
	Nothing for me.	

3.
| What do you like best for | breakfast? |
| | lunch? |

4.
| I like | eggs | more than anything. |
| | pizza | |

5.
| Do you like . . . more than . . . ? |

6.
| Of course! . . . is my number one favorite. |

7.
| What is your favorite | vegetable | in the whole world? |
| | fruit | |

8.
| That's my favorite, too. |
| . . . is the best! |
| That's not my favorite. |
| I like . . . even more than . . . . |

Words and Expressions

boil	drain	ground	medium	shredded
buttermilk	dressing room	ground beef	nothing	simmer
cereal	fill	honey	pancakes	strawberries
chocolate	flakes	instead	pepper	taco shells
corn	French toast	jam	poultry	toast
cumin seed	fridge	lettuce	rare	try on
dairy products	garlic powder	lightly	sausage	uncovered
diced	grapefruit	maple syrup	scrambled	well done
dish	grated	marmalade	seasonings	would

in the whole world   number one favorite
more than anything   start with

Communication Points
Ask and talk about quantity

THINGS YOU CAN COUNT

How many apples do we have?

We have There are	a few some a lot of	apples. pears. peanuts. cookies. sandwiches.
We don't have There aren't	any	

Do we have Are there	a lot of any	apples? cookies?

THINGS YOU CAN MEASURE

How much milk do we have?

We have There is	a little some a lot of	milk. tea. sugar. coffee. popcorn.
We don't have There isn't	any	

Do we have Is there	a lot of any	milk? popcorn?

1. **You and your partner are planning a party for about 20 people. You have some of the things for the party, but you probably need more. You look at the picture above. Your partner checks the party list. Ask and answer with your partner. Then change roles.**

   A: Do we have a lot of cookies?
   B: No. We only have a few. We need some more.
   A: Do we have any popcorn?
   B: Yes, we have a lot of popcorn.
   A: Is there any ice cream?
   B: No, there isn't. We need to get some.

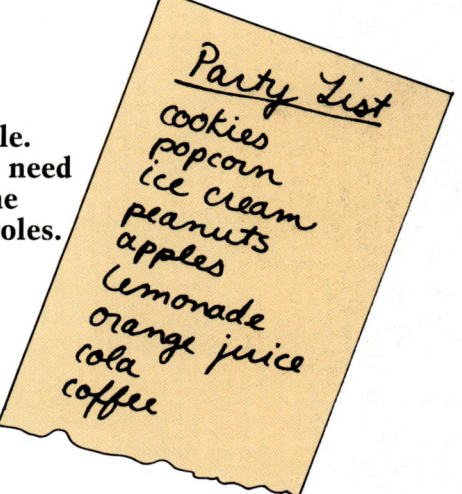

Party List
cookies
popcorn
ice cream
peanuts
apples
lemonade
orange juice
cola
coffee

BACK TO SCHOOL 63

2. **Interview your partner. Ask questions, using the words below.**

friends	jewelry	CDs
homework	free time	housework to do
pets	books at home	paper in your notebook

> A: Do you have many friends?
> B: Yes, I have a lot of friends.

> A: Do you have much homework tonight?
> B: No, I don't have any homework.

Identify people and places

1. **Can you identify the people and places in the photos? Copy and complete the sentences below, using these names and places: *William Shakespeare, Neil Armstrong, New York, Paris, San Francisco, Christopher Columbus.***

   a. The city that has the Eiffel Tower is . . . .
   b. The author who wrote Hamlet was . . . .
   c. The city that has the Golden Gate Bridge is . . . .
   d. The person who discovered America was . . . .
   e. The first person who walked on the moon is . . . .
   f. The city that has the Empire State Building is . . . .

2. **Check your answers with your partner.**

> A: What's the city that has the Eiffel Tower?
> B: (Give your answer.)

> A: Who was the author who wrote Hamlet?
> B: (Give your answer.)

3. Ask your partner what people do. Use the information below.

> A: What does a photographer do?
> B: A photographer is a person who takes photos.

photographer	delivers letters
pilot	plays tennis
taxi driver	drives a taxi
mail carrier	designs buildings
folk singer	takes photos
tennis player	works in a hospital
babysitter	writes books
architect	takes care of children
author	flies a plane
nurse	sings folk songs

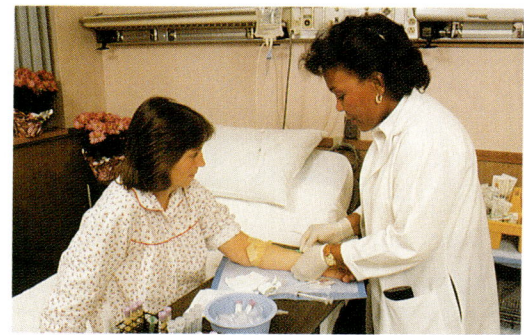

BACK TO SCHOOL

Language Points
Reading an interview

SCHOOL LIFE IN THE UNITED STATES

REPORTER: Well, let's start with your name and age.
RUTH: I'm Ruth Wilson and I'm fourteen.
REPORTER: So you're in high school, aren't you?
RUTH: Yes, I'm a ninth grader at Hamilton High.
REPORTER: Do you take a lot of different subjects?
RUTH: The usual stuff—math, social studies, science, English, and my elective, Spanish.
REPORTER: What do you like best?
RUTH: Well, we're doing maps in social studies. That's cool. We're learning how to draw them, and we're going to learn about surveying land.
REPORTER: What about your English class?
RUTH: Right now we're reading *The Mayor of Casterbridge*. I don't like it much. It's all about England a long time ago. But we just finished *The Pearl* by John Steinbeck, and that was great.
REPORTER: What about extra curricular activities?
RUTH: I play basketball—I play center.
REPORTER: That must take a lot of your time.
RUTH: Yeah, but I really like it.
REPORTER: Is your school very big?
RUTH: Let's see, there are about 800 kids in the whole school.
REPORTER: What about your classes—how many students are usually in a class?
RUTH: About twenty or a few more.
REPORTER: Do you get a lot of homework?
RUTH: Well, I don't personally get a lot, maybe an hour or an hour and a half. But some kids get three hours every night.
REPORTER: What if you were having a hard time in school? Is there anybody you can go and talk to about it?
RUTH: Oh, sure, there's a guidance counselor. He'll help you if you want to change a class or if you're in trouble with your work.
REPORTER: What hours are you at school?
RUTH: It starts at 7:45 and gets out at 2:15. On Wednesdays we get out early, at 1:20.
REPORTER: How long are class periods?
RUTH: They're about 40–50 minutes. But you don't have the same schedule every day.
REPORTER: How do you feel about school in general?
RUTH: Well, I don't really like going to school, but it's something that you have to do. I usually enjoy it.

> **GLOSSARY**
> **hav**·ing a hard time—finding problems in your life
> stuff—things
> sur·**vey**·ing—measuring land spaces, often for buying and selling

Read the passage. On your paper, make a chart like this and fill in the information about Ruth's school. Then work with a partner to fill in the information about your own school.

	RUTH'S SCHOOL	YOUR SCHOOL
a. number of students in the school	???	???
b. number of students in a class	???	???
c. hours of school each day	???	???
d. minutes for each class	???	???
e. number of subjects taken		
f. names of subjects		
g. hours of homework per night		

Writing

How is your school similar to Ruth's? How is it different? Write a paragraph describing the similarities and differences using information from your chart in exercise 1.

Reading and writing schedules

RUTH'S SCHOOL SCHEDULE

Block Time	Monday	Tuesday	Wednesday	Thursday	Friday
A 7:45- 7:55	HOMEROOM	HOMEROOM	HOMEROOM	HOMEROOM	HOMEROOM
B 8:00- 8:50	ENGLISH	GYM	FREE BLOCK	GYM	FREE BLOCK
C 8:55- 9:40	FREE BLOCK	FREE BLOCK	ENGLISH	FREE BLOCK	ENGLISH
D 9:45-10:30	FREE BLOCK	ENGLISH	GYM	FREE BLOCK	SCIENCE
E 10:35-11:20	SPANISH	SPANISH	SPANISH	SPANISH	SPANISH
F 11:25-11:45	LUNCH	LUNCH	LUNCH	LUNCH	LUNCH
G 11:50-12:30	ALGEBRA	ALGEBRA	ALGEBRA	ALGEBRA	ALGEBRA
H 12:35- 1:20	SOCIAL STUDIES	SCIENCE	FREE BLOCK	SCIENCE	SOCIAL STUDIES
I 1:25- 2:15	SCIENCE	SOCIAL STUDIES	EARLY RELEASE	SOCIAL STUDIES	FREE BLOCK

1. **Answer these questions about Ruth's school schedule.**
   a. How many subjects does Ruth study?
   b. When does she have lunch?
   c. How many times a week does she have gym? English?

2. **Write your own school schedule on a piece of paper. Work with your partner and compare your schedules with Ruth's. Make a list of similarities and differences between your schedule and Ruth's.**

THE SCHOOL YEAR

FIRST SEMESTER

Starts the first week of September.
Ends before December 25th.
Holidays include: Columbus Day (October),
   Veterans Day and Thanksgiving (November).
Christmas Vacation: 10 days.

SECOND SEMESTER

Starts the first week of January.
Ends at the end of June.
Holidays include: Martin Luther King Day (January),
   Presidents Day (February), Memorial Day (May).
Spring Vacation: 1 week in April.

3. **Answer these questions about Ruth's school year.**
   a. How many vacation days are in each semester?
   b. When does summer vacation begin? When does it end?
   c. How many weeks do students study in each semester?

4. **Write your own school year schedule on a piece of paper. Then answer the questions of exercise 3 about your school year. Be ready to discuss the similarities and differences between your school year and Ruth's.**

Listening

Listen to Ruth's homeroom teacher announcing some changes in Ruth's schedule for Monday and Tuesday. Note the changes on your paper.

Practice Points

1. **Copy and complete the sentences with *much* or *many* on your paper.**

   a. There isn't . . . cheese in the refrigerator.
   b. There aren't . . . cookies left.
   c. How . . . pizza did he eat?
   d. He doesn't work . . . hours a day.
   e. Were . . . people at the party?
   f. I don't like . . . sugar on my cereal.

2. **Copy and complete these sentences with *a little* or *a few*.**

   a. I ate . . . carrots at dinner last night.
   b. I only had . . . meat.
   c. I bought . . . flowers yesterday.
   d. There's only . . . milk left.
   e. Do you have . . . minutes to help me?
   f. There were only . . . people there.
   g. Most of the oranges are bad, but there are . . . good ones left.

3. **Copy the following sentences, filling in the blanks with *any* or *some*.**

   a. Is there . . . milk? Yes, there's . . . .
   b. What about . . . coffee this morning?
   c. Are there . . . apples in the kitchen? No, there aren't . . . .
   d. I don't have . . . money. I'm broke.

4. **Copy and complete these sentences. The first one is done for you.**

   a. . . . sings folk songs.

   A folksinger is a person who sings folksongs.

   b. . . . flies a plane.
   c. . . . takes care of children.
   d. . . . writes books.
   e. . . . takes photos.
   f. . . . plays tennis.
   g. . . . designs buildings.
   h. . . . drives a taxi.
   i. . . . delivers letters.

5. **On your paper, combine these sentences to make one sentence. The first two are done for you.**

   a. The city is New York. New York has a lot of skyscrapers.

   The city that has a lot of skyscrapers is New York.

   b. The boy is on the football team. The boy is playing with John.

   The boy who is playing with John is on the football team.

   c. The teenagers are Bill and Carol. They live in New York.
   d. The lady is Miss Bennett. She is Tim's aunt.
   e. The band wants to become famous. They played last night.
   f. The book is "Touchdown." It really teaches football.

Let's Rock!

Turn to page 128.
Listen to the song *Busy, Busy, Busy*.
Read the words as you listen. Then sing along!

Check Points

Communication Points

Ask and talk about quantity
Do we have a lot of cookies? No, we only have a few.
Is there any ice cream? No, there isn't.

Identify people and places
What's the city that has the Eiffel Tower?
Who was the author who wrote Hamlet?
A photographer is a person who takes photos.

1.
How many	apples cookies	do we have?
How much	milk popcorn	

2.
Do we have Are there	a lot of any	apples? cookies?
Do we have Is there	a lot of any	milk? popcorn?

3.
We have There are	a few some a lot of	apples. cookies.
We don't have There aren't	any	

4.
We have There is	a little some a lot of	milk. popcorn.
We don't have There isn't	any	

5.
	many	friends? pets?
Do you have	much	homework? free time?

6.
What's the city	that	has the Eiffel Tower?
Who was the author	who	wrote Hamlet?

7.
The city	that	has the Eiffel Tower	is Paris.
The author	who	wrote Hamlet	was Shakespeare.

8.
What does a	photographer pilot	do?

9.
A	photographer	is a person who	takes photos.
	pilot		flies a plane.

Words and Expressions

architect	deliver	mail carrier		
athlete	design	nurse		
author	discover	peanuts		
babysitter	folk-singer	pocket	11th grade	11th form
band	folk song	taxi	peanuts	ground nuts
become	housework	teenager	private school	public school
born	jewelry	take care of	public school	county school
carrots	journalist		vacation	holiday

Present   **Past**
write   wrote

BACK TO SCHOOL

10 WHERE SHOULD WE GO?

KENJI: Tim! Guess what!
TIM: What?
KENJI: My mother is taking Janet and me to London for a week. She's going to a business conference, so we're going to tour the city while she's busy.
TIM: That's great! What are you going to see there?
JANET: Well, actually, we don't know yet. Could you give us some ideas?
TIM: Of course! If the weather is nice the first day, why don't you go to Buckingham Palace?
KENJI: That's where we can see the Changing of the Guards.
TIM: Right!
JANET: Where should we go if it rains?
TIM: You could go to the National Gallery. It's one of the best art galleries in the world!
KENJI: Well, I really don't like art galleries.
TIM: Then how about going to Madame Tussaud's Wax Museum? It's incredible. You can see all of these famous people, life size, made of wax.
KENJI: Okay, let's go there.
TIM: By the way, I hope you are going to take a really big suitcase.
JANET: Why?
TIM: So I can fit in it and go with you!

Communication Points
Ask for and give suggestions
Agree or disagree

1. Read the chart below with your partner.

Ways of asking for suggestions:	
What should we do?	
What can we do?	
Where should we go?	
Ways of giving suggestions:	
Let's	Let's go to Kew Gardens.
We could	We could bring our lunch.
What about	What about a picnic?
Why don't	Why don't we get something to eat?
How about	How about a trip on the Thames?
Ways of agreeing and disagreeing:	
That's a good idea.	I'm sorry, but I don't like . . . .
Okay.	No, I don't want . . . .
Sure, let's go there.	No, not . . . .
Yes, let's do that.	Well, I really don't like . . . .

2. Pretend you are in London. What would/wouldn't you like to see/do/eat/drink? Make a chart like the one below. Fill in with *yes* or *no*.

		YES/NO
BEAUTIFUL DAY?	**Places to see:**	
	The Tower of London	???
	The Houses of Parliament	???
	Sherlock Holmes's House	???
	Trafalgar Square	???
	Madame Tussaud's Wax Museum	???
BORED?	**Things to do:**	
	Take a trip on the Thames	???
	Have a picnic at Greenwich	???
	Spend an afternoon at the amusement park	???
HUNGRY?	**Things to eat:**	
	fish and chips kippers	
	hot dog scones	
	pizza Stilton cheese	
THIRSTY?	**Things to drink:**	
	cola milk	
	orange squash English tea	
	lemonade	

WHERE SHOULD WE GO?

A: It's a beautiful day. Let's go out.
I'm bored. Let's do something exciting.
I'm hungry. Let's eat something.
I'm thirsty. Let's get something to drink.

B: Where should we go?
What could we do?
What should we eat/drink/have?

A: Let's go to . . . .   Why don't we go to . . . ?
Let's have . . . .   Why don't we have . . . ?

B: That's a great idea!   No, I don't like . . . .   What about . . . ?
Okay.   No, not . . . .   We could . . . .
Yes, let's go there.   I'm sorry, but I don't . . . .   Let's . . . .
Yes, let's have . . . .   Why don't we . . . ?

3. Choose sentences from the box above. Make dialogues like the one below, giving suggestions for things to do in London.

A: It's a beautiful day. Let's go out.
B: Where should we go?
A: Let's go to the Tower of London./Why don't we go to the Tower of London?
B: That's a great idea./No, not there. What about the Houses of Parliament?

The Tower of London from the Thames River

4. Make a chart like the one below. Then fill it in with at least two suggestions for each column of things to do in your town or city.

Sports or activities to watch or play	Places of interest to go to	Movies or plays to go to see	Other things you want to do
???	???	???	???

5. Use your chart to ask and answer with your partner. Use expressions from the box at the top of the page.

A: I'm bored. Let's do something exciting.
B: What could we do?
A: Why don't we . . . ?
B: . . . .

Language Points
Reading advertisements

Read the three tours of London. Which tour would you take if:

1. you wanted to see the Crown Jewels?
2. you only had the morning free?
3. your only free day was Sunday?
4. you also wanted to see the Albert Hall?
5. you wanted an all day tour?
6. you wanted to visit Sherlock Holmes's house?

CITY
Includes all admission charges
Adult £3.70   Child £2.50

Tour of the City of London which passes the Mansion House and Monument.

Visits to St. Paul's Cathedral (an alternative Wren Church on Sundays) and the Tower of London are included. Also the Crown Jewels are visited if exhibition is open.

Starting from Victoria Coach Station at 2:00, back at 4:00. Daily, including Sundays, April 2 - October 16.

WESTMINSTER
Adult £3.00   Child £2.25

Tour of Westminster Abbey and West End with the principal sights of London, including the Houses of Parliament, Trafalgar Square, Marble Arch, Sherlock Holmes's House and Piccadilly Circus.

A visit to the Changing of the Guard is also included (provided that it is taking place on the day of the tour). Starting from Victoria Coach Station at 9:00, back at 12:00. Mondays to Saturdays, April 2 - October 15.

LONDON DAY TOUR
Includes a light lunch and admission charges   Adult £6.50   Child £4.90

An introduction to all London's principal sights including Marble Arch, Albert Hall, the Houses of Parliament, St. Paul's Cathedral, the Tower of London, Westminster Abbey, Trafalgar Square, Buckingham Palace, the Changing of the Guard, Cleopatra's Needle, and the Wax Museum.

A light lunch in a London Pub is included. Starting from Victoria Coach Station at 10:00, back at 5:00. Mondays to Saturdays, April 2 - October 15.

Role play

Pretend you are in London. Make a list of five or ten places you will visit. Discuss your list with your partner. These questions may help you.

1. What will you see first?
2. Where will you go then?
3. When will you eat lunch?
4. Who/What will you see?

Reading for information

GENERAL FACTS

NAME OF BUILDING   The Houses of Parliament.
LOCATION   In London, near the River Thames.
DESCRIPTION   Famous Gothic-style buildings designed by Sir Charles Barry together with Big Ben clock tower.
AGE   Present buildings date from 1852 and are part of a Royal Palace built in 1050.

POINTS OF INTEREST

The House of Commons and the House of Lords meet daily.
The Houses of Parliament are visited by thousands of tourists every year.
Different parts of the Houses of Parliament can be visited:
The Central Lobby
The Robing Room
The House of Commons (from Strangers' Gallery)

Visitors can hear debates (from 2:30 P.M.).

HOURS AND COST OF ADMISSION

SUMMER   Thurs.–Sat. 9:30 A.M. to 5 P.M.   ADMISSION: free
WINTER   Thurs.–Sat. 9:30 A.M. to 4 P.M.

Copy and complete the following paragraph. Use the information above.

The Houses of Parliament are in ..., ... the River .... These ... were built in ... and were designed by .... The present buildings are part of a ..., built in ... ... of tourists visit the Houses of Parliament .... They can visit the ..., the ..., and the .... The Houses of Parliament are open ... 9:30 A.M. ... 5 P.M. ... Thursday through ... in the ..., and until 4 P.M. in the .... The admission is ....

Writing

Now write about a place or a building you know. Remember to give:

a. general facts { name of the building / where it is / what it is like }

b. points of interest { what it is used for / what it has / what visitors can see / what visitors can do there }

c. hours and cost of admission

Listening

A tour guide is showing some tourists around London. Listen to her speech. On your paper write down the places they see on the tour. Then guess which of the tours on page 73 the tourists are following.

Reading fiction

From *THE SPECKLED BAND* by Sir Arthur Conan Doyle

This reading is from a story by Sir Arthur Conan Doyle, who began writing stories about the brilliant detective Sherlock Holmes and his assistant Dr. Watson in the late 1880s.

In *The Speckled Band*, we find Sherlock Holmes and Dr. Watson living in a boarding house in London. One morning Holmes is told that there is a strange woman waiting for him in the sitting room.

"Good morning, madam," said Holmes cheerily. "My name is Sherlock Holmes. This is my intimate friend and associate, Dr. Watson, before whom you can speak as freely as before myself. Ha! I am glad to see that Mrs. Hudson has had the good sense to light the fire. Pray draw up to it, and I shall order you a cup of hot coffee, for I observe that you are shivering."

"It is not cold which makes me shiver," said the woman in a low voice, changing her seat as requested.

"What, then?"

"It is fear, Mr. Holmes. It is terror."

"You must not fear," said he soothingly, bending forward and patting her forearm. "We shall soon set matters right, I have no doubt. You have come in by train this morning, I see."

"You know me, then?"

"No, but I observe the second half of a return ticket in the palm of your left glove. You must have started early, and yet you had a good drive in a dogcart, along heavy roads, before you reached the station."

The lady gave a violent start and stared in bewilderment at my companion.

"There is no mystery, my dear madam," said he, smiling. "The left arm of your jacket is spattered with mud in no less than seven places. The marks are perfectly fresh. There is no vehicle save a dogcart which throws up mud in that way, and then only when you sit on the left-hand side of the driver."

"Whatever your reasons may be, you are perfectly correct," said she. "I started from home before six, reached Leatherhead at twenty past, and came in by the first train to Waterloo."

GLOSSARY
be·**wil**·der·ment—not understanding
com·**pan**·ion—person with you, friend
dog·cart—a small 2 wheeled carriage pulled by a horse
mud—soft wet earth
ob·**serve**—notice, see
re·**quest**·ed—asked
shiv·er·ing—shaking, little quick movements
vi·o·lent start—sudden strong movement

Answer these questions on your paper.

a. How many people are in the room?
b. Was it a cold or warm morning? How do you know?
c. Was the woman shivering because she was frightened or because she was cold?
d. How did Holmes know that the woman came by train?
e. How did he know that she also took a dogcart?

WHERE SHOULD WE GO?

Practice Points

1. Look at the chart for exercise 1 on page 71. Then look for examples of giving suggestions in the unit dialogues of Units 2, 3, 4, 6, 8, and 9. Write the examples from the dialogues on your paper.

2. Look at the chart you made for exercise 4 on page 72. Write four dialogues asking and giving suggestions. Use the expressions in the box at the top of page 72.

Let's Rock!

Turn to page 130.
Listen to the song *No, No, No*.
Read the words as you listen. Then sing along!

Check Points

Communication Points

Ask for and give suggestions — What should we do? Where should we go? Let's go to Kew Gardens./What about a picnic?

Agree or disagree — That's a good idea./Sure, let's go there. I'm sorry, but I don't like. . . ./No, I don't want. . . .

1.
What	should can could	we	do?
Where	should		go?

2.
Why don't we	go to Kew Gardens?
How about What about	a picnic? a trip on the Thames?

3.
Let's We could	go to Kew Gardens. get something to drink.

4.
That's a good idea. Okay.		
Sure, Yes,	let's	go there. do that.

5.
I'm sorry, but I don't like. . . . No, I don't want. . . . No, not. . . . Well, I really don't like. . . .

Words and Expressions

activities   bored   square   spend an afternoon
amusement park   could   tower

amusement park   fun fair

Communication Points
Report what people are asking

1. **Ask and answer about pictures *a–d*.**

   A: What is Tom asking Alice?
   B: He's asking who they are.

2. **Ask and answer about pictures *e–h*.**

   A: What does Becky want to know?
   B: She wants to know if Mario is Italian.

Report what people are saying

Complete and practice the dialogues with your partner.

Report people's commands and requests

a. Laurie — Joan
b. Peter — Ted
c. Mr. White — Will
d. Mrs. Lopez — Betsy
e. Mrs. Howard — Chris
f. Don — Mrs. Tanaka
g. Mr. Gold — Donna
h. David — Mike

1. Ask and answer with your partner about pictures *a–d*.

> A: What did Joan tell Laurie yesterday?
> B: She told her to turn on the light.

> A: What did Mr. White tell Will yesterday afternoon?
> B: He told him not to play baseball.

2. Ask and answer with your partner about pictures *e–h*.

> A: What did Mrs. Howard ask Chris last night?
> B: She asked him to turn off the TV.

> A: What did Mr. Gold ask Donna last Saturday?
> B: He asked her not to come home too late.

Language Points

Open dialogue

Talk to John on the telephone. Paulo is with you.

YOU: ....
JOHN: Hi. This is John.
YOU: ....
JOHN: Listen, would you like to go to the baseball game?
YOU: ....
JOHN: Why don't you ask Paulo if he wants to come?
YOU: .... (talk to Paulo)
PAULO: Sorry, but I'm meeting a friend in half an hour.
YOU: .... (talk to John)
JOHN: Well, tell him he can bring his friend, too.
YOU: .... (talk to Paulo)
PAULO: Okay. I'll tell him.
YOU: .... (talk to John)
JOHN: Fine. I'll call you back later. Bye!
YOU: ....

Listening

1. **Listen to Kenji talking to Miss Bennett about his vacation in London. Look at the chart below and write on your paper the words and phrases Kenji uses to talk about London, the weather, the food, and the people.**

LONDON	WEATHER	FOOD	PEOPLE
1. dirty	1. changeable	1. delicious	1. reserved
2. clean	2. fair	2. boring	2. unfriendly
3. messy	3. not too cold in winter	3. awful	3. rude
4. neat	4. not too warm in summer	4. healthy	4. friendly

2. **Use the words and phrases to write a few notes on Kenji's impressions. Start like this: Kenji says that London . . . . .**

Telephone message game

Work in groups of 7 or 8 people. Each group forms a line. The first student in each line whispers a command or a request to the second one. The second student then has to whisper what he/she heard to the next student, and so on until the last student has to say aloud what he/she has heard. The first student in the line will then say aloud his/her original message.

EXAMPLE

A (*whispers to* B): Go to the blackboard and write the name of your favorite baseball team.

B (*whispers to* C): A asked me to go to the blackboard and write the name of my favorite baseball team.

C (*whispers to* D): A asked B to go to the blackboard and write the name ..., etc.

AN INVITATION

Prince Naruhito and Masako Owada on their wedding day.

Reading a biography
MASAKO OWADA: THE 21ST CENTURY PRINCESS

Masako Owada is perhaps the most well-known Japanese woman in the world, and for good reason. She is the future empress of Japan, the world's oldest monarchy. Owada's marriage to Crown Prince Naruhito was one of the biggest events in Japan's recent history. The entire nation turned on their TVs on June 9, 1993 to watch a computer-generated simulation of the private Shinto ceremony and about 200,000 people cheered as the new princess and her husband made their way to their home, the Togu Palace.

Masako Owada is not a traditional princess by any stretch of the imagination. Born in 1963, her parents taught her and her twin sisters the value of a good education. Owada studied hard and was a good student. She graduated from Harvard University in 1985 and went on to Oxford University. She lived abroad for many years. The daughter of a prominent diplomat, she also had a successful career at the Ministry of Foreign Affairs. Many people believed that she would become an ambassador one day. She was a rising star and was in a prime position to become a very important and successful international businesswoman. In fact, in 1990 she received a big promotion to the North American division of the Ministry. Marriage to a crown prince did not seem to be in her plans.

As Owada was busily shaping her career, Prince Naruhito was seeking a wife. In October, 1986, Masako-san, as she is affectionately known, was invited to an afternoon tea at the palace and met Prince Naruhito there. She was just one of 40 women selected by the Imperial Household Agency, the bureaucracy that manages all of the royal family's affairs. Some say that the prince knew that Owada was the perfect choice to be his wife. They saw each other on occasion over the years and Owada even turned down two marriage proposals from the prince.

Eventually the prince's quest for a bride was successful and Owada agreed to marry him. Many people were very surprised by her decision since she had expressed great concern about becoming a member of the royal family. The new princess felt, rightfully so, that she would be giving up her freedom by marrying the prince. She didn't particularly like the idea of becoming such a public figure, but after careful consideration, she opted to marry Prince Naruhito. Upon her engagement in December, 1992, Owada made a statement: "I would be lying if I said I had no sad feelings about leaving the foreign ministry, but I felt that my role now was to accept the proposal from the prince and make myself useful in my new life in the imperial household."

Masako Owada saying goodbye at the Foreign Ministry.

All eyes will be on this royal marriage. People are wondering if Masako Owada, the former careerwoman, will influence the Japanese monarchy. Many Japanese women feel a certain rapport with the princess; others feel sorry for her since she will have to change her lifestyle drastically. In any event, both Masako and Naruhito will ultimately be the ones to lead Japan in the 21st century.

> **GLOSSARY**
> **em·press**—wife of an emperor; a royal leader
> **sim·u·la·tion**—the act of imitating or representing something
> **prom·i·nent**—widely known
> **dip·lo·mat**—a person who speaks for his/her country in its relations with foreign countries
> **am·bas·sa·dor**—important government official
> **af·fec·tion·ate·ly**—lovingly
> **bu·reau·cra·cy**—government administration
> **con·sid·er·ation**—careful thought
> **mon·ar·chy**—government ruled by one person

1. **Read the passage. Then take notes on the important information about Masako Owada's life. Write your notes on your paper.**

2. **Use the notes you have prepared to talk with your partner about Owada's life.**

3. **Answer the questions on your paper.**
    a. What kind of career did Owada have? What do you think she wanted to do with her life?
    b. What do you think Prince Naruhito's life was like? Why do you think he had to find a wife?
    c. Why were people surprised when Owada agreed to marry the prince?
    d. Why do you think Owada was sad to leave her job at the foreign ministry?

4. **What do you think life is like as part of a royal family? Would you like it? Why or why not? Describe a typical day as a member of a royal family. Compare ideas with your partner.**

AN INVITATION

Practice Points

1. Write what each person is saying.

a. Bill: I'm cold.

Bill says that he's cold.

b. Tim: I have to leave at 6:00.
c. Mr. Cooper: I have a headache.
d. Kenji and Janet: We can't watch TV tonight.
e. Police officer: You can ride bicycles here.
f. Paulo: I won't forget to lock the door.
g. Carol: I'll clean my room.
h. Sue and Barbara: We saw Carlos jogging yesterday afternoon.
i. Diana: I want to go to the movies.
j. Mr. and Mrs. Day: We will see you on Saturday.

2. Write sentences using *told* or *asked*.

a. Don't break the vase. (Mrs. Cooper/John)

Mrs. Cooper told John not to break the vase.

b. Can you close the door, please? (Bill/Carol)

Bill asked Carol to close the door.

c. Can you turn on the light, please? (Mr. Day/Mrs. Day)
d. Do your homework. (Mrs. Cooper/John)
e. Don't play football in the road. (a police officer/Mike)
f. Can you pass the sugar, please? (Tim/Miss Bennett)
g. Don't drive so fast, please. (Barbara/Carlos)
h. Remember to lock the front door. (Miss Bennett/Paulo)
i. Don't forget to mail my letters. (Janet/Mrs. Koga)

3. Write sentences using *want to know*.

a. How many brothers do you have? (Tim/Janet)

Tim wants to know how many brothers Janet has.

b. Are they coming on Monday? (Mr. Day/the Coopers)

Mr. Day wants to know if the Coopers are coming on Monday.

c. How much sugar do you put in your coffee? (Miss Bennett/Mrs. Cooper)
d. How did you get to the Tower of London? (Tim/Bill)
e. Can you ride a bicycle? (Peter/Mike)
f. Do you like English food? (Mr. Cooper/John)
g. Why are you driving so fast? (Barbara/Carlos)
h. Will you go for a walk after dinner? (Mr. Day/Mrs. Day)
i. What are you going to do on Friday? (Sue/Barbara)
j. Do you want to go to a pop concert? (Chris/Laura)

Check Points

Communication Points

Report what people are asking	What is Tom asking Alice? He's asking who they are.
Report what people are saying	Mom wants to know if you're ready to go. I'll be ready in five minutes. He says (that) he'll be ready in five minutes.
Report people's commands and requests	What did Joan tell Laurie yesterday? She told her to turn on the light. What did Mrs. Howard ask Chris last night? She asked him to turn off the TV.

1.
What is	Tom	asking	Alice?
	Mrs. Banks		Ann?

2.
He's	asking	who they are.
She's		why she's crying.

3.
What does	Becky	want to know?
	Mrs. Thomas	

4.
She	wants to know if	Mario is Italian.
		Mr. Brown lives in Chicago.

5.
Mom	wants to know if	you're ready to go.
Tom		you can go with us.

6.
I'll be ready in five minutes.
Well, I can't go tonight.

7.
He	says (that)	he'll be ready in five minutes.
She		she can't go tonight.

8.
What did	Joan	tell	Laurie	yesterday?
	Mrs. Howard	ask	Chris	last night?

9.
She	told	her	to turn on the light.
	asked	him	to turn off the water.

Words and Expressions

loudly   turn on
turn off   vase

Present	Past
tell	told

Communication Points
Ask and talk about past events

1. Match the questions with the answers. Then find the matching picture.

QUESTIONS

a. Hey, Tom, what happened to your hand?
b. Maria was alone last night. Did she have dinner?
c. Mr. Lopez, you went to the movies yesterday, didn't you? Did you enjoy yourself?
d. Did you hear about the big fire at the state park?
e. Where was Tran?
f. Ann, what did you and Judy buy yourselves?
g. Did you leave the children by themselves last night?

ANSWERS

h. Oh, yes. She cooked herself a very good dinner.
i. Yes, the firefighters couldn't control it. They let it burn itself out.
j. I cut myself with a knife.
k. He was studying by himself at the library.
l. Yes, they were fine. They looked after themselves. They are old enough now.
m. I sure did. I enjoyed myself a lot. I saw a great western.
n. We bought ourselves new running shoes.

1.
2.
3.
4.
5.
6.
7.

2. Now ask and answer with your partner.

> A: Hey, Tom, what happened to your hand?
> B: I cut myself with a knife.

MAKING ARRANGEMENTS 87

Invite people
Arrange to meet people

1. Practice the following dialogue with your partner.

A: Would you like to go to the zoo?
B: Mmm. That sounds great. How can we get there?

A: Let's go by bus.
B: Okay. And where should we meet?

A: How about at the bus stop?
B: Okay. What time?

A: Should we make it ten o'clock?
B: Ten o'clock at the bus stop. That's fine. Bye!
A: Bye!

2. Look at the pictures on page 89. Invite your partner to go to one of the places shown. Arrange how to get there, where to meet, and what time. Then change roles.

WHERE . . . ?	beach	swimming pool	theater

HOW . . . ?	by car	on foot	by subway

WHERE . . . ?	at the corner of Main Street and Walnut	in front of your house	outside the subway station
WHAT TIME . . . ?			

3. **Work with your partner. Make arrangements to go somewhere in your town. Arrange how to get there, where to meet, and what time to be there.**

MAKING ARRANGEMENTS

Ask for and give information

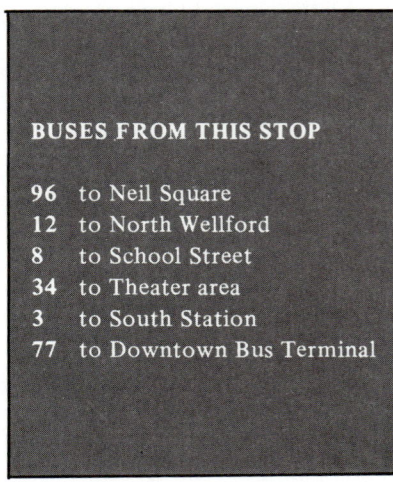
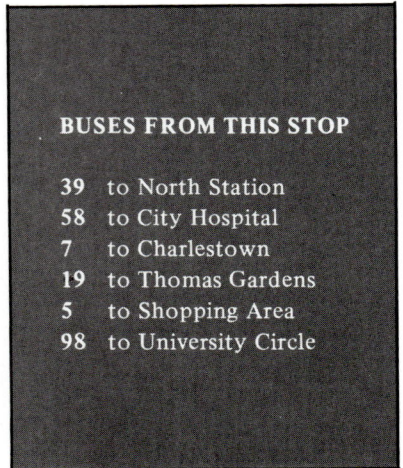

BUSES FROM THIS STOP

96 to Neil Square
12 to North Wellford
8 to School Street
34 to Theater area
3 to South Station
77 to Downtown Bus Terminal

BUSES FROM THIS STOP

39 to North Station
58 to City Hospital
7 to Charlestown
19 to Thomas Gardens
5 to Shopping Area
98 to University Circle

1. **MEMORY:** Look at one of the bus stop signs for one minute and memorize bus numbers and destinations. Your partner will memorize the other sign. Then close the book and try to write down as many bus numbers and destinations as you can. Open your books and check your answers.

2. Ask and answer questions like the ones below.

   A: Excuse me. Is this the right bus stop for . . . ?
   B: Yes, that's right./No, I'm afraid this isn't the bus stop you want.
   A: Which bus goes to . . . . ?
   B: Sorry, I don't know./Sorry, I have no idea./You want bus number . . . .
   A: Thank you very much./Well, thank you anyway.

Language Points
Reading for pleasure
A COLLEGE OF CLOWNS

1. To skim is to glance through a passage quickly to get the main idea. When you skim, you don't read every word. Skim the story that follows for one minute. Then choose the sentence which best describes the main idea of the passage.

   a. Clown students come from many different places and backgrounds.
   b. Clown College trains people to be clowns for the circus.
   c. There are not many young clowns in the circuses.
   d. Many people want to be clowns.

A COLLEGE OF CLOWNS

"Clowning around" is serious business at the Ringling Brothers and Barnum & Bailey Clown College. About a thousand hopeful future clowns have gone through this school, and some of them have been chosen to become clowns in the Ringling Brothers and Barnum & Bailey Circus, "The Greatest Show on Earth."

The school wants to preserve the skills that in the past were handed down from old clown to young clown in the circus. The Clown College was started in 1968, when the Circus found that it had only fourteen clowns and they were all in their 50s. Now there are always young clowns in training at Clown College. They hope they will be among the lucky graduates who are chosen to join the circus.

During the ten week session at Clown College students work very hard. They spend eight hours a day, six days a week, learning clown skills. They take courses in clowning, pantomime, juggling, stilt walking, makeup, unicycling, making props, making costumes, acrobatics, and others. They learn to create a clown personality that is their own, with its own makeup, costume, and funny routines.

The students at Clown College come from all over the United States and from many different backgrounds. All the students want to be able to make people happy. One young juggler said, "Being a clown means making people laugh and forget their troubles."

When the classes are all finished, the college hopes that the new clowns will have a special kind of magic. Their magic is not the usual kind of magic tricks, but a way to reach out to everyone with imagination in the wonderful world of the circus.

GLOSSARY
back·ground—all of someone's life, family, schooling, and where they live
hand·ed down—given or taught by an older person to a younger person
pre·**serve**—save, keep
ses·sion—length of time during which there are classes
skill—knowing how to do a difficult thing
spe·cial—not ordinary, different

2. **Read the passage. Write the answers to the questions on your paper. Then discuss your answers with your partner.**
   a. Why did the Ringling Brothers and Barnum and Bailey Circus start Clown Collge?
   b. How long do students study at Clown College? How many hours a day do they study?
   c. Name five things that students study in the program.
   d. Clown students come from many different backgrounds, but they all want to be clowns for the same reason. What is the reason?
   e. Are you a "clown" sometimes? What can you do to make people laugh? Can you do tricks, pantomime (act out something without speaking), juggle, or do acrobatics?
   f. In many countries, clowns are different from the clowns you see in these pictures. What does a typical clown look like in your country? Write a short description or draw a picture of one.

Listening

Three friends are making plans for the weekend. Listen to the dialogue, and write on your paper where they decide to go, how they are going to go, when they will meet, and where they will meet.

Practice Points

1. **Write a dialogue following the instructions given on the right.**

CARLOS:	.... (Greet Barbara.)
BARBARA:	.... (Respond to greeting.)
CARLOS:	.... (Ask what she is doing this evening.)
BARBARA:	.... (Say you aren't doing anything special.)
CARLOS:	.... (Invite Barbara to go to the movies.)
BARBARA:	.... (Accept. Ask what is on.)
CARLOS:	.... (Say there is a good mystery at the Odeon.)
BARBARA:	.... (Say you like mysteries.)
CARLOS:	.... (Arrange to meet Barbara in front of the theater.)
BARBARA:	.... (Say okay. Ask what time.)
CARLOS:	.... (Arrange to meet Barbara at six-thrity.)
BARBARA:	.... (Say okay. Ask Carlos not to be late.)
CARLOS:	.... (Promise you won't be late. Say goodbye.)
BARBARA:	.... (Say goodbye.)

2. **You are in New York, and you want to take a bus to the Empire State Building. You don't know where the bus stop is. Write a dialogue in which you ask people for information. Follow the instructions given on the right.**

   YOU: .... (Ask if this is the right bus stop for the Empire State Building.)
   MAN: .... (He says he doesn't know.)
   YOU: .... (Thank the man. Ask a woman the same question.)
   WOMAN: .... (She says this isn't the bus stop you want.)
   YOU: .... (Ask where the bus stop is.)
   WOMAN: .... (She says it is over there.)
   YOU: .... (Ask which bus goes to the Empire State Building.)
   WOMAN: .... (She says you want the number eleven.)
   YOU: .... (Thank her. Say goodbye.)
   WOMAN: .... (Responds.)

3. **Complete the sentences below. Use one of these pronouns: *myself, yourself, himself, herself, itself, ourselves, yourselves, themselves.***

   a. "Goodbye! Take care of . . . !"
   b. She did all the homework by . . . .
   c. I wasn't worried about . . . . I was worried about you!
   d. He hurt . . . when he fell down the stairs.
   e. We drove to New York by . . . .
   f. She often talks to . . . when she is alone.
   g. Did you and Bill hurt . . . badly?
   h. Let me introduce . . . . I'm Jim Brandon.
   i. The students can listen to . . . on tape.
   j. The machine turns . . . off.
   k. Thanks for the party. We enjoyed . . . very much.
   l. They painted the house by . . . .
   m. The dog can open the door by . . . .

Let's Rock!

Turn to page 131.
Listen to the song *Weekend*.
Read the words as you listen. Then sing along!

Check Points

Communication Points

Ask and talk about past events	Hey, John, what happened to your hand? I cut myself with a knife.
Invite people Arrange to meet people	Would you like to go to the zoo? That sounds great. How can we get there? Let's go by bus. And where should we meet?
Ask for and give information	Excuse me. Is this the right bus stop to Neil Square? Yes, that's right./No, you want bus number ninety-six.

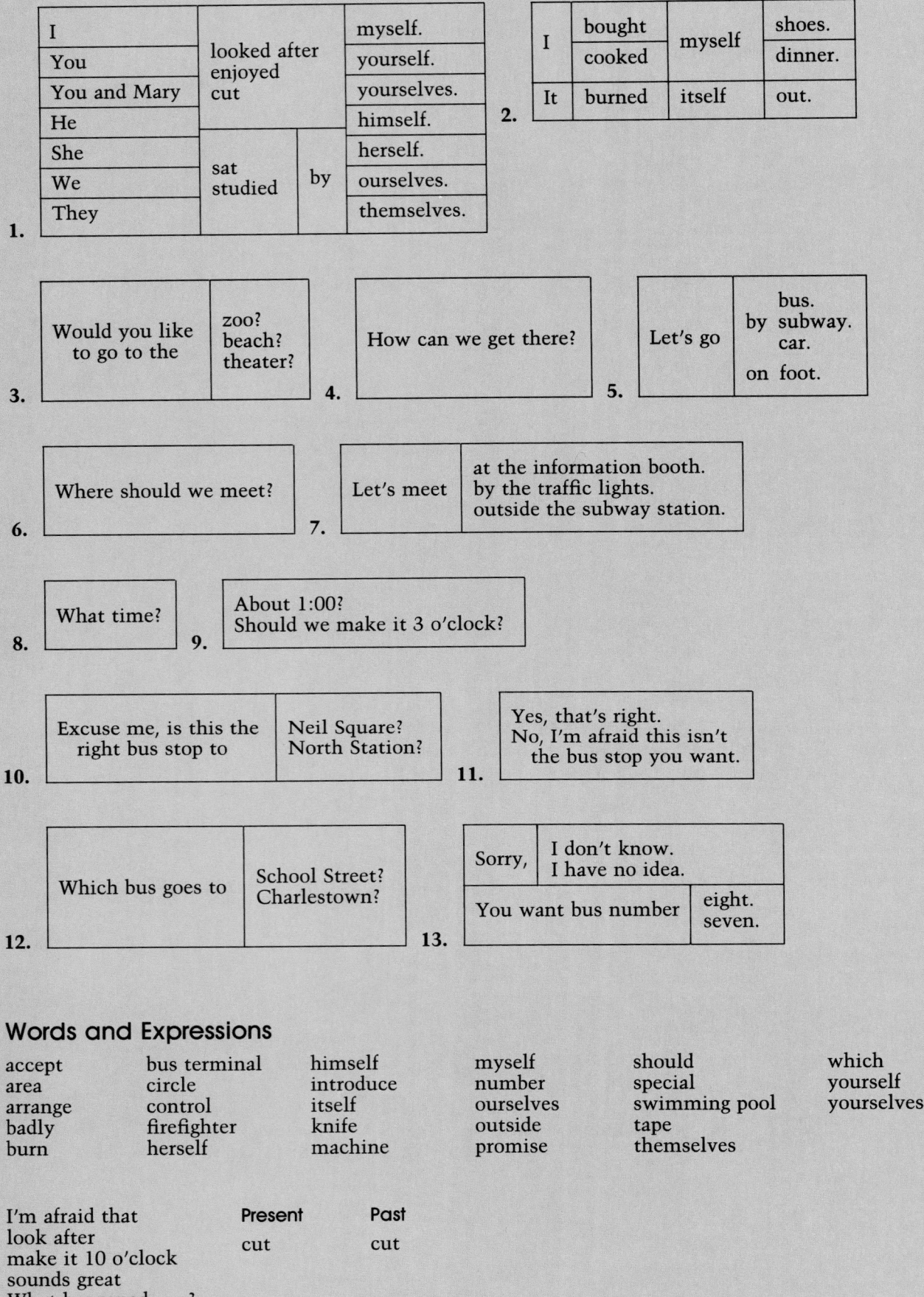

Words and Expressions

accept	bus terminal	himself	myself	should	which
area	circle	introduce	number	special	yourself
arrange	control	itself	ourselves	swimming pool	yourselves
badly	firefighter	knife	outside	tape	
burn	herself	machine	promise	themselves	

I'm afraid that
look after
make it 10 o'clock
sounds great
What happened . . . ?

Present	Past
cut	cut

Communication Points

Express opinions

Express preferences

Agree or disagree

HOW TO EXPRESS:

Opinions	Preferences	Disagreement	Agreement
I think it's exciting.	I'd rather go see the computers.	I don't like it.	Neither do I.

1. **Look at the chart. Four sentences from the dialogue on page 95 have been classified on it. Under which heading would you put each of the following sentences?**

   a. I don't think so.
   b. I'd rather stay home.
   c. So would I.
   d. So do I.
   e. Golf is boring and costs a lot of money.
   f. Boring? Nonsense.

2. **Check the classifications with your partner and discuss your own choices.**

3. **Write ten sentences expressing your opinion on the following topics. Here are some words you can use:** *boring, dangerous, delicious, difficult, exciting, expensive, noisy, old, quiet, scary, too easy.*

   football

   a. football
   b. Western movies
   c. big cities
   d. small towns
   e. flying
   f. museums
   g. checkers
   h. hamburgers
   i. rock music
   j. classical music
   k. English class
   l. homework

4. **Compare your opinions from exercise 3 with your partner.**

   > A: I think football is very exciting.
   > B: So do I./I don't. I think it's boring.

5. **Ask your partner questions following the example.**

   > A: Which is more exciting—playing football or playing basketball?
   > B: I think . . . is more exciting.

   a. exciting—playing football/playing basketball
   b. fun—dancing/listening to music
   c. interesting—math/history
   d. difficult—English/science
   e. delicious—chocolate ice cream/strawberry ice cream
   f. expensive—living in New York City/living in Mexico City
   g. (Make up questions of your own like these.)

Language Points
Reading about science

FIREWORKS TO FIRE DRAGONS: EARLY CHINESE INVENTION

Most people know that the Chinese people invented fireworks. Each year we are reminded of this on Chinese New Year's Day when the sound of firecrackers is heard in Chinese communities all over the world.

The Chinese people invented much more than fireworks, however. Take food, for example. Did you know that the Chinese invented spaghetti, macaroni, and noodles? When we think of spaghetti, most of us think of Italy. But the Italians learned about it from people who traveled in China.

The ancient Chinese invented many other things that we use today. They invented the wheelbarrow and the compass. They even invented paper and printing.

These were all fairly simple inventions. But Chinese scientists and engineers also made very complicated things. To learn about the stars and planets, they made a planetarium which showed how the sky looked at night. To indicate when and where earthquakes were taking place, they invented a seismograph, or earthquake measuring instrument. This instrument, built more than 1,800 years ago, was a beautiful bronze bowl with eight dragons around its sides. Each dragon had a wooden ball in its mouth. When there was an earthquake, the ball fell out of the mouth of the dragon on the side of the bowl where the earthquake was. Even an earthquake that was so far away that no one could feel it would make the ball fall out of the dragon's mouth.

The Chinese used gunpowder to make more than 30 kinds of fire arrows for war. One kind, the "fire dragon," was a two-stage ballistic missile! Four booster rockets strapped to the "dragon" sent it flying. As it neared its goal, the rockets lit a group of fire arrows that shot out of the dragon's mouth to set enemy ships on fire.

The next time you eat spaghetti, or guide yourself with a compass, or watch a 4th of July fireworks show, say a word of thanks to the Chinese people who invented these things thousands of years ago. Maybe there is "nothing new under the sun."

A wheelbarrow

The seismograph

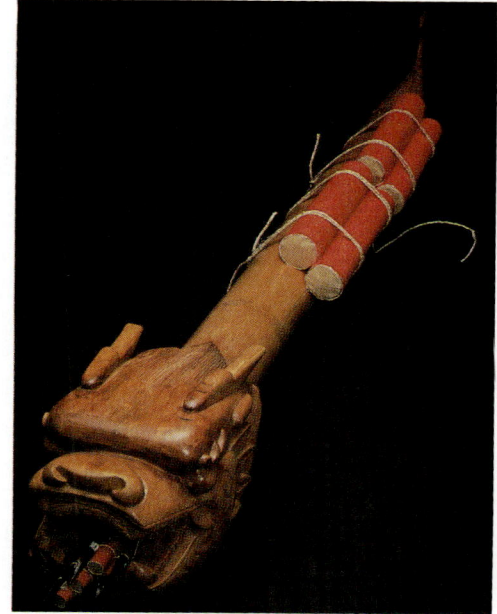
The fire dragon

AT THE SCIENCE EXHIBIT

1. **Scan the passage and find the vocabulary words listed below on the left. Read the sentences where they are used to understand the general meaning. Then match the words with the definitions on the right.**

   a. seismograph
   b. planetarium
   c. fireworks
   d. gunpowder
   e. earthquake

   f. a strong shaking or moving of the earth's surface
   g. displays of colors and noise produced by gunpowder
   h. a device to measure the strength, time, and place of an earthquake
   i. a place to show a representation of the solar system
   j. a very explosive mixture of chemicals

2. **Copy the sentences below. Fill in the blanks with vocabulary from the list above.**

   a. China has many strong . . . , which damage buildings and houses and cause deaths.
   b. The early . . . helped Chinese scientists tell where and when an earthquake occurred.
   c. The Chinese used . . . to shoot rockets at enemy ships in battles.
   d. A . . . was invented to study the skies and stars.
   e. . . . , which use gunpowder, were invented by the Chinese and are used on the 4th of July.

Writing

Go to your school library and find out about some important inventions of the 1800s and 1900s. How did these inventions change people's lives? Take your notes in English. Then work with your partner and write a paragraph reporting what you find out.

Listening

Mark Chen, his wife Lynn, and their sixteen year old son Carl are talking about life in big cities and small towns. Take notes on what they say. Then answer these questions on your paper.

1. Where does Lynn want to live? Why?
2. Does Mark agree or disagree?
3. What's Carl's opinion? Why?

Reading fiction
DOWN THE RABBIT HOLE*

Alice was beginning to get very tired of sitting by her sister on the bank, and of having nothing to do: once or twice she had peeped into the book her sister was reading, but it had no pictures or conversations in it, "and what is the use of a book," thought Alice, "without pictures or conversations?"

So she was considering, in her own mind (as well as she could, for the hot day made her feel very sleepy and stupid), whether the pleasure of making a daisy-chain would be worth the trouble of getting up and picking the daisies, when suddenly a white rabbit with pink eyes ran close by her.

There was nothing so very remarkable in that; nor did Alice think it so very much out of the way to hear the Rabbit say to itself, "Oh dear! Oh dear! I shall be too late!" (when she thought it over afterwards, it occurred to her that she ought to have wondered at this, but at the time it all seemed quite natural); but when the Rabbit actually took a watch out of its waistcoat-pocket, and looked at it, and then hurried on, Alice started to her feet, for it flashed across her mind that she had never before seen a rabbit with either a waistcoat-pocket, or a watch to take out of it, and, burning with curiosity, she ran across the field after it, and was just in time to see it pop down a large rabbit-hole under the hedge.

In another moment down went Alice after it, never once considering how in the world she was to get out again.

GLOSSARY
con·**si**·der—think about
dai·sy—a flower, usually with long white petals and a yellow center
dai·sy chain—a chain or necklace made of daisies
get tired of—be bored
it oc·**curred** to her—she thought
peep **in**·to—take a quick look
re·**mark**·able—very unusual
start·ed to her feet—got up quickly

*From *Alice's Adventures in Wonderland* by Lewis Carroll.

1. **Read the passage from *Alice's Adventures in Wonderland* and take notes on the following:**
   a. What was Alice doing at the beginning of the story?
   b. What animal did she see?
   c. What was strange about the animal?
   d. What did Alice do?

2. **Are these sentences true or false? Write them on your paper. If a sentence is false, correct it to make it true. When you finish you will have a summary of the story.**
   a. Alice was bored because she had nothing to do.
   b. Her sister was reading an interesting book.
   c. It was a hot day and Alice felt sleepy and lazy.
   d. Suddenly she saw a white dog with green eyes.
   e. Alice was very surprised to hear the rabbit say, "Oh dear! Oh dear! I shall be too late."
   f. Alice jumped up when she saw the rabbit take a watch out of its pocket and look at it.
   g. She ran after the rabbit and saw it go down a large hole.
   h. Alice didn't go down the hole after the rabbit.

3. **Now practice summarizing the story in your own words. Close your book and tell the story to your partner. Then change roles.**

4. **Do you know the story of *Alice's Adventures in Wonderland*? If so, can you tell some of the things that happen to Alice after she goes down the hole? If you don't know the story, can you imagine one of Alice's adventures? Tell your classmates.**

5. **If you want to know something about Lewis Carroll's life, write these sentences in order to form a complete paragraph.**

   Lewis Carroll, A Short Biography
   a. Then he wrote other books, nonsensical poems, and parodies.
   b. He never married, but he was very fond of children and spent much of his time with them—the Alice stories were originally written for the young daughters of Dr. Liddell, the Dean of Christ Church College.
   c. Charles Dodgson died in 1898.
   d. In 1861 he became a deacon at the church.
   e. Lewis Carroll was the pen name of the Rev. Charles Lutwidge Dodgson.
   f. His first book, *Alice's Adventures in Wonderland*, was published in 1865.
   g. Born in 1832, he was educated at Rugby and at Christ Church College, Oxford, where he spent the rest of his life as lecturer in mathematics.

Practice Points

1. Read the examples and charts. Then copy and complete the responses in column B.

| A: I'm not English. | A: I don't speak Chinese. |
| B: Neither am I. | B: Neither do I. |

| A: Tim didn't go. | A: I like English. |
| B: Neither did I. | B: So do I. |

| A: Mario is Italian. | A: I can drive. |
| B: So am I. | B: So can I. |

| Neither | do / did / am / can / have | I. |

| So | do / did / am / can / have / would | I. |

          A   **B**

a. I'm busy tonight.   a. So . . . I.
b. I don't feel too well.   b. Neither . . . I.
c. He can't ice skate.   c. Neither . . . I.
d. I haven't done my homework.   d. Neither . . . I.
e. I want to go to the movies.   e. So . . . I.
f. He didn't like the food.   f. Neither . . . I.
g. Peter said it was a good movie.   g. So . . . I.
h. I can speak English.   h. So . . . I.
i. I'd rather go to the concert.   i. So . . . I.
j. Ana has been to New York City.   j. So . . . I.
k. I'm not very tired.   k. Neither . . . I.

2. Look at the examples and charts above. Then write similar responses to the statements using *neither* or *so*.

a. Pedro is a student.
b. I did not study last night.
c. Tim speaks English.
d. Barbara doesn't like tests.
e. I ate pizza last night.
f. I do not have an American car.
g. I can speak English.
h. I cannot speak Spanish.
i. Janet is not from New York.
j. Bill hasn't been to Tokyo.
k. I'd rather see the computers.

3. Agree or disagree with the following statements. Use *neither, so, I don't .... I like/hate ....*

a. I like soccer.
b. I hate milk.
c. I love doing my homework.
d. I don't like this exercise!
e. My mother hates rock music.
f. I like getting up early in the morning.
g. Tim thinks living in the U.S. is exciting.
h. I like going shopping with my parents.
i. I prefer guitar music to piano music.
j. I don't like children under five years old.

Check Points

Communication Points

Express opinions — I think it's exciting.
Express preferences — I'd rather go see the computers.
Agree or disagree — I don't like it./Neither do I.

1.
| I don't speak Chinese, |
| Tim didn't go. |
| I'm not English. |
| He can't ice skate. |
| I haven't done my homework. |

2.
Neither	do	I.
	did	
	am	
	can	
	have	

3.
| I like English. |
| Peter said it was a good movie. |
| Mario is Italian. |
| I can drive. |
| Ana has been to New York City. |
| I'd rather go to the concert. |

4.
So	do	I.
	did	
	am	
	can	
	have	
	would	

5.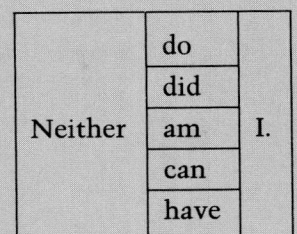

6.
| I don't think so. |
| I don't like it. |

7.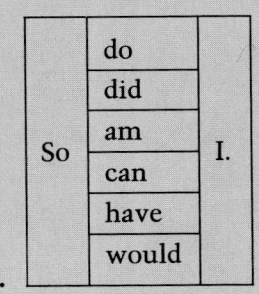

Words and Expressions

| easy | neither | scary | I'd rather |
| ice skate | noisy | tests | I don't feel well |

102 UNIT THIRTEEN

A TRIP TO THE RACES 14

CARLOS: Hi, Barbara!
BARBARA: Oh, hi Carlos! Did you have a good day?
CARLOS: Yeah. Say, Barbara, I've just had an idea.
BARBARA: Oh, really? What is it?
CARLOS: Have you ever been to a car race?
BARBARA: No. As a matter of fact, I have a brother who lives near Sundown Park. I visited him for a whole week, but I never went to the races!
CARLOS: When was that?
BARBARA: Last April.
CARLOS: Well, how would you like to go? There's a big race there next Saturday, and the editor wants me to write an article about Nell Chambers. If she wins this race, it will be big news. Maybe you can stay with your brother.
BARBARA: That's a great idea!
CARLOS: How long does it take to get there by car?
BARBARA: It takes about four hours... But isn't your car being repaired?
CARLOS: Yes, but I thought we could rent a car or go by bus.
BARBARA: Oh, let's go by bus. It's more relaxing, and it's cheaper, too.
CARLOS: Good idea. Why don't you call your brother tonight and let him know you're coming?

Communication Points
Ask and talk about your experiences

1. Make a chart like the one below. Add these items to your chart: *on a plane? to the dentist? in a tent? in a hotel? on a picnic with your friends? to a disco? on a roller coaster?* Answer the questions about yourself.

Have you ever been ...	YOU		YOUR PARTNER	
	Yes/No	When?	Yes/No	When?
to a circus?	Yes	last summer	No	
in a hospital?				
on a ship?				
abroad?				

2. Now ask and answer with your partner and fill in your partner's answers on your chart.

> A: Have you ever been to a circus?
> B: Yes, I have.
> A: When was that?
> B: Last summer./In 19 . . . .

> A: Have you ever been in a hospital?
> B: No, I haven't./No, I've never been in one.

3. Make two charts like the one below—one for you and one for your partner. On your chart, write at least five places you have been to, how long you were there, and when you went there.

What places have you been to?	How long?	When?
Paris	3 days	1993

4. Now ask and answer with your partner and fill in your partner's answers.

> A: What places have you been to?
> B: I've been to . . . .
> A: How long did you stay?
> B: . . . days./. . . weeks.
> A: And when were you there?
> B: . . . .
> A: Where else have you been?
> B: I've been to . . . .

Ask and talk about time

Copy the chart and write your guesses.

Questionnaire	YOU	YOUR PARTNER
How long does it take to go by plane from New York to:		
Rome?		???
London?	???	???
Lisbon?	???	
Tokyo?	???	
Rio de Janeiro?		
Buenos Aires?		
Mexico City?		

2. **Ask and answer with your partner. Write the guesses on your chart.**

> A: How long does it take to go from New York to Rome by plane?
> B: About . . . hours, I think.

3. **Check your guesses with the answers at the bottom of this page.**

4. **Answer these questions about yourself.**

How long does it take you:
   to get dressed?   to go to school?
   to brush your teeth?   to do your homework?
   to have breakfast?   to walk to your friend's house?

5. **Work in groups of three. Ask and answer the questions.**

> A: How long does it take you to get dressed?
> B: It takes me . . . .
> C: How long did he/she say it takes him/her to get dressed?
> A: He/she said it takes . . . .

Answers to exercise 1, page 105: Rome, about 9 hours; London, about 6½ hours; Lisbon, about 6½ hours; Tokyo, about 18 hours; Rio de Janeiro, about 8 hours; Buenos Aires, about 11½ hours; Mexico City, about 5 hours.

Language Points
Reading for information

1. **Read the brochure "Around Japan" and take notes on the following. Copy the chart and fill in the information on your paper.**

	HOTEL	TIME OF ARRIVAL	PLACES TO VISIT
Nagoya	???	???	???
Kyoto	???	???	???
Osaka	???	???	???
Kobe	???	???	???
Hiroshima	???	???	???

SHIBA TOURS AROUND JAPAN

Tour Number 577 – an 8 Day Scenic Tour, with English-speaking guides

From **Tokyo** to **Nagoya, Kyoto, Osaka, Kobe,** and **Hiroshima**

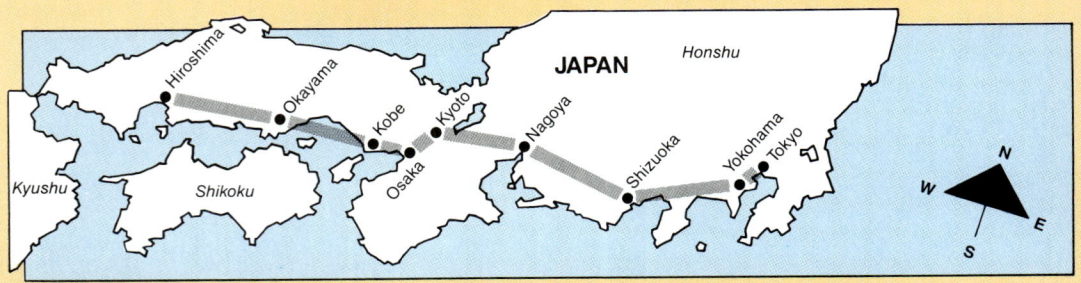

1st Day:
Tokyo to Nagoya on the "bullet train" (shinkansen), through Kawasaki on Tokyo Bay, the port city of Yokohama, and Shizuoka. Arriving in Nagoya at about 8 P.M. for supper and overnight at Asakusa Hotel.

2nd Day:
Sightseeing tour of the city, including visits to the textile industry and the pottery industry. Afternoon train to Kyoto, arriving at about 7 P.M. Dinner and overnight at the Imperial Hotel.

3rd Day:
Sightseeing tour of Kyoto, visiting the Golden Pavilion, Nijo Castle, Katsura Imperial Villa, and Sento Imperial Palace.

4th Day:
Kyoto to Osaka, arriving at about 9:30 A.M. Tour of the city including Osaka Castle, famous bridges across canals and rivers, and shopping in the underground shopping centers. Dinner and overnight at the Sumida Hotel.

5th Day:
Osaka to Kobe, arriving at about 2 P.M. for tours of the port and shipbuilding, followed by visits to several Buddhist temples. Dinner and overnight at the Honshu Hotel.

6th Day:
Free morning in Kobe. Then train from Kobe to Hiroshima, arriving at around 5:30 P.M. Dinner and overnight at the Mori Hotel.

7th Day:
Sightseeing tour of Hiroshima, including visits to the Peace Memorial Museum and Park.

8th Day:
Return train from Hiroshima to Tokyo, arriving in Tokyo at about 7:30 P.M.

Departs:
8:45 A.M. from Tokyo Station. Departures on Wed., March-June, and Sat. July-October. Tour does not operate November through February.

Special tours available with German, French, or Spanish speaking guides. Ask for separate brochure.

Price: $500 except for the month of September – $650
Price includes transportation, entrance fees, all meals, hotel rooms.

2. Read the brochure again and write the answers to these questions on your paper.

a. Where do they go the first day?
b. Are there tours starting on Thursday? On Wednesday?
c. How long does it take to get from Tokyo to Nagoya?
d. What do they visit in Nagoya?
e. When do they visit the Golden Pavilion?
f. Where is the Golden Pavilion?
g. When they arrive in Osaka, do they have dinner before or after a sightseeing tour of the city?
h. Where are the visits to Buddhist temples?
i. At what time of year is the tour more expensive?
j. Where do the tours start?
k. Is an English-speaking guide included in the tour?
l. How many days is the complete tour?

Writing

Imagine you work in a travel agency. Prepare a tour similar to the Japanese tour for the region where you live. The tour must last at least four days. If you can, draw pictures of the places on the tour.

Listening

Maria is asking questions at the Kyoto Tourist Bureau. These are the notes she wrote down. Copy her notes and fill in the missing information on your paper.

Golden Pavilion—temple covered with . . . , burned down in . . . , first built in . . . , signs in . . . tell history
Free guides—. . . from Kyoto University
Imperial Palace—famous . . . , made in . . . , closed every . . .
National Museum—pottery from about . . . B.C., open from . . . to . . .
Shopping—small . . . near . . . station, get Shopping Guide . . . of Kyoto for fans, pottery, . . . , and dolls

Practice Points

	Ann and Bob	Mr. Banks	Frank	Lisa
Canada		1992	1993	1994
France		1989	1990	1993
Venezuela	1992	1990		

1. **Use the chart to write questions and answers on your paper, using *has, hasn't, have, haven't, ever, been, was,* and *were*. Follow the pattern of the examples.**

   a. Lisa/Canada

   Has Lisa ever been to Canada?

   Yes, she has.

   When was she there?

   In 1994.

   b. Ann and Bob/France

   Have Ann and Bob ever been to France?

   No, they haven't.

   c. Frank/France
   d. Mr. Banks/Venezuela
   e. Lisa/Venezuela
   f. Ann and Bob/Canada
   g. Frank/Canada

2. **Write four dialogues that you practiced with your partners in exercise 5 on page 105.**

3. **Look at the bus schedule below. Then write four questions and answers about the schedule. The first one is started for you.**

   Buses from New York City

TO	DEPART FROM NYC	ARRIVE
Boston, MA	7:30 a.m.	12:00 noon
Pittsburgh, PA	8:30 a.m.	6:00 p.m.
Albany, NY	11:00 a.m.	1:30 p.m.
Washington, DC	1:30 p.m.	6:30 p.m.

   How long does it take to go from New York to...?

Check Points

Communication Points

Ask and talk about your experiences
Have you ever been to a circus?
Yes, I have. When was that? Last summer./In 1993.
No, I haven't./No, I've never been to one.

Ask and talk about time
How long does it take you to get dressed?
It takes me. . . .
How long did she say it takes her to get dressed?
She said it takes her. . . .

1.
| Have you ever been | in a hospital? |
| | to a circus? |

2.
Yes,	I have.	
	I haven't.	
No,	I've never been	in one.
		to one.

3.
| What places have you been to? |

4.
I've been to	London.
	Paris.
	New York.

5.
| How long did you stay? |

6.
| Three | days. |
| | weeks. |

7.
| When were you there? |
| When was that? |

8.
| In 1993. |
| Last summer. |

9.
| How long | does | it take you | | | to get dressed? |
| | did | he / she | say | it takes | him / her | to go to school? |

10.
| He / She | said it takes | him / her | an hour. |

Words and Expressions

circus
ever
roller coaster

Present	Past	have/has +
am/is/are	was/were	been

A TRIP TO THE RACES

Communication Points
Ask and talk about recent activities

Think about the past ten days. How have you spent your free time?

A	B
1. Have you been to the movies?	1. What did you see? When?
2. Have you bought any CDs?	2. What did you buy? Where? When?
3. Have you watched TV?	3. What did you watch? What time?
4. Have you seen any relatives?	4. Who did you see? When? Where?
5. Have you read a new book?	5. What was it about?
6. Have you written a letter?	6. Who did you write to?
7. Have you eaten out in a restaurant?	7. Where did you go? What did you have?
8. Have you invited anyone home?	8. Who did you invite? Why? When?
9. Have you played any sports?	9. What did you play? When? Who with?
10. Have you done anything interesting?	10. What did you do?
11. Have you gone anywhere interesting?	11. Where did you go?

1. **Answer the questions in column A about yourself. Write the number and *yes* or *no* on your paper. If the answer is *yes*, answer the question in column B, also.**

2. **Ask your partner about his or her recent activities. Ask the questions in column A. If the answer is *yes*, ask the questions in column B.**

> A: Have you been to the movies recently?
> B: Yes, I have.
> A: What did you see?
> B: I saw . . . .
> A: When did you see it?
> B: . . . .

3. **Look at Carol's and Bill's schedules for last week. Ask and answer with your partner.**

> A: Has Carol done her book report?
> B: Yes, she has.
> A: When did she do it?
> B: Last Monday.

	MON.	TUES.	WED.	THURS.	FRI.	SAT.	SUN.
Carol	Write book report	Read French book	French club	Basketball practice	Eat dinner at Diana's		
Bill	Do science report	Soccer practice	Movies with Tim	Store - pants and socks	Write letters	Soccer game	

Language Points

Listening

Copy the form on your paper. Listen to the telephone conversation and fill in the information on your paper.

```
AIRLINE RESERVATION

Destination  _____???_____

Day  _____???_____          Departure time  _____???_____

Arrival time  _____???_____

RETURN TRIP

Day  _____???_____          Departure time  _____???_____

Connection  _____???_____   Arrival time  _____???_____


Passenger's name  _____???_____   Fare  _____???_____
```

Reading for pleasure
SIDEBOTTOM

1. These paragraphs are not in the correct order. Put them in order so that you have a joke.

   a.   The next morning, when Sidebottom came down to breakfast again, the Frenchman was there. "Bon appétit," the Frenchman said again. Sidebottom was a bit surprised to hear his name again, but he did the same, "Sidebottom." This happened every morning for a week.

112   UNIT FIFTEEN

b. Realizing his mistake, Sidebottom rushed into the restaurant. The Frenchman was sitting at his usual table. Sidebottom sat down opposite him. "Bon appétit," he shouted. The Frenchman looked at him and smiled. "Sidebottom," he replied.

c. An Englishman was visiting Paris for the first time. He was staying at a hotel in the center of the city. He went down to breakfast on the first day, and sat at the same table as a Frenchman. The Frenchman was eating croissants and drinking coffee. The Englishman ordered the same. When the croissants arrived, The Frenchman smiled and said, "Bon appétit." "That must be his name," thought the Englishman. He smiled back and said his own name, "Sidebottom."

d. At the end of the week, a friend of Sidebottom's arrived from England. "I'm having a marvelous time," he said. "I met a very nice Frenchman. His name is Bon Appétit."—"That isn't his name," said the friend. "That's what the French say before they eat something!"

> **GLOSSARY**
> a bit sur·**prised**—a little surprised
> crois·**sant**—a French roll
> **mar**·vel·ous—wonderful
> mis·**take**—something done wrong
> **re**·al·iz·ing—understanding for the first time
> re·**plied**—answered

2. **Answer these questions on your paper.**
   a. Where is the Englishman staying?
   b. Where does the Englishman meet the Frenchman?
   c. Does the Englishman speak French? Does the Frenchman speak English? How do you know?
   d. What did the Englishman think the Frenchman was saying to him when he said, "Bon appétit"?

3. **Do you know a joke or funny story you can tell in English? Tell it to your partner.**

Practice Points

1. **Look at the chart of Carol's and Bill's schedules on page 111. Follow the example dialogue in exercise 3 on that page and write two dialogues about Carol and two dialogues about Bill.**

2. **Copy and complete the sentences on your paper.**
   a. . . . you seen any good movies lately?
      Yes, ... I . . . the new Clint Eastwood movie on Saturday.
   b. What . . . you do last Monday? I . . . gymnastics practice.
   c. . . . he . . . a letter to his grandparents? Yes, ... He wrote them last week.
   d. When did you . . . those new shoes? I . . . yesterday.
   e. . . . Jane and Susan . . . their homework? Yes, ... They did it . . . .
   f. . . . she . . . her dinner. No, ... She's going to eat later.
   g. Where did you . . . last weekend? We . . . to the beach.

3. Use your answers to the questions on page 111 and write a letter to your friend. Say what you have done recently.

Dear ...,
I have a lot of things to tell you because I have been very busy recently. I have been out every night this week! I went to the movies and saw .... I have also seen some relatives. ...

OR

Dear ...,
I don't have much to tell you because I haven't been very busy recently. I have done my homework, but I haven't ....

Check Points

Communication Points

Ask and talk about recent activities

Have you been to the movies recently?
Have you bought any CDs recently?
Have you done anything interesting recently?

1.
Have you	bought	any CDs		recently?
	seen	any relatives		
	gone	anywhere	interesting	
	done	anything		

2.
Yes,	I have.
No,	I haven't.

3.
What	did you	buy?
		do?
Who		see?
Where		go?

4.
I	bought	....
	saw	
	went	

5.
When did you	buy	it?
	see	them?
	go	there?

6.
Has	Carol	done her homework?
	Bill	written his book report?

7.
Yes,	she has.
No,	he hasn't.

Words and Expressions

anyone
gymnastics
practice
recently
relatives

Present	Past	have/has +
invite	invited	invited
play	played	played
watch	watched	watched
am/is/are	was/were	been
buy	bought	bought
do	did	done
eat	ate	eaten
go	went	gone
read	read	read
see	saw	seen
write	wrote	written

NELL'S VICTORY 16

CARLOS: Nell! Nell! Can I ask you a few questions?
NELL: Sure. But I have to be in the winner's circle in a few minutes.
CARLOS: Okay, I'll make it fast. First of all, congratulations! It was a terrific race.
NELL: A terrific one, but a close one!
CARLOS: It's the first time a woman has won here at Sundown Park. You must be very happy.
NELL: I sure am! I've raced here for three years, you know. . . .
CARLOS: But not with this fabulous car!
NELL: That's right. I've only been driving this car since March.
CARLOS: You've done a great job in such a short time.
NELL: Thanks.
CARLOS: How long have you been driving race cars?
NELL: Well, I used to drive go-carts when I was a girl, but I've been driving professionally since 1982.
CARLOS: What are your plans for the future?
NELL: My plans? Relax . . . for at least a week. And then get ready for the next race in Germany.
CARLOS: Well, good luck. And congratulations again!
NELL: Thanks.

Communication Points
Ask and talk about people's lives

Carlos talked to Nell Chambers before the race and took these notes.

```
Nell Chambers
1962 — Born in Philadelphia.
1973 — Started driving go-carts.
1979 — Graduated from Philadelphia Central High School.
1990 — Moved to New Jersey.
1992 — Started driving professionally.
1993 — Joined Larssen team.
March this year — Started driving new race car.
```

1. **Copy and complete this dialogue on your paper using the information above. Then read the dialogue with your partner.**

   CARLOS: How long have you been living in . . . ?
   NELL: Well, I've been living there since 1990. Before that I lived in . . . .
   CARLOS: So you've been living there for . . . years. And how long have you been driving professionally?
   NELL: . . . since . . . .
   CARLOS: Oh, so you've been driving professionally for . . . years?
   NELL: That's right.
   CARLOS: And when did you join the Larssen team?
   NELL: . . . .

2. **Write some important dates and events in your life. Then trade papers with your partner. Ask and answer questions like those in the dialogue in exercise 1.**

3. **Read the notes on the next page, and match them with the pictures. Then ask and answer questions like the ones below with your partner.**

   A: How long has Bill Day been . . . ?
   B: He has been . . . since . . . ./He has been . . . for . . . years.
   A: When did Barbara Cruz . . . ?
   B: She . . . in . . . .

116 UNIT SIXTEEN

Barbara Cruz

1953 was born in Washington, D.C.
1968 bought first camera, began taking pictures
1976 moved to New York
1983 started own company, Light Write

Bill Day

1979 was born in San Francisco
1983 moved with family to Riverdale
1987 began taking piano lessons
1988 began reporting for the school newspaper

Janet Koga

1978 was born in Brooklyn Heights
1988 started playing soccer with friends
1990 joined school baseball team
1991 began studying Spanish in school

Walter Cooper

1973 was born in San Antonio, Texas
1976 moved to Riverdale with her family
1989 started playing the guitar
1992 met Carlos and began dating him

4. Now interview your partner. Ask him/her how long he/she has been:

    a. living in this town
    b. studying English
    c. attending this school
    d. studying in this class
    e. using this book
    f. playing . . .

Ask and talk about past habits

Have you ever	NEVER	USED TO	STILL
...driven go-carts?	???	???	???
...played with dolls?	???	???	???
...drunk milk before going to bed?	???	???	???
...eaten lollipops?	???	???	
...collected model cars?	???		
...read fairy tales?	???		
...written a diary?	???		
...watched cartoons on TV?	???		

1. Make a chart like the one above. Mark your answers.
2. Talk to your partner. Ask and answer like this:

> A: Have you ever driven go-carts?
> B: No, I've never driven go-carts in my life.
> *or*
> Well, I used to drive go-carts, but I don't do that anymore.
> *or*
> Yes, I have. And I still drive go-carts.

Language Points
Reading about people
SHIRLEY MULDOWNEY
DRAG CAR RACER

Shirley Muldowney has been racing cars a long time. She says, "There were all those people telling me that I couldn't do this, or that I shouldn't do that." But she didn't pay any attention to all that advice, and she has become one of the best drag car racers in the world.

Her life has been a history of firsts. In 1965 she was the first woman to be licensed by the National Hot Rod Association (NHRA). Ever since that time she has been driving professionally. In 1975 she was the first woman to break the six-second barrier (going from zero to 250 miles per hour in less than six seconds). In 1977 Muldowney was the first woman to win the Winston World Championship, and when she won it again in 1980 she was the first driver, male or female, to win it twice. She was the first woman driver to be chosen for the ten member All American auto racing team. And in 1982 she became the first driver to ever win the NHRA championship title for the third time.

When she was a teenager, her boy friend built a souped-up car, but he was afraid to drive it really fast. But Shirley, at five foot four and 120 pounds, wasn't afraid. And she says about racing, "at the track a lot can go wrong... In that small space of time [before a race], you become comfortable in the car and apprehension fades. Just before you step in, that's when your guts go crazy, but it's not because of fear, it's because you want to win."

A movie of Shirley Muldowney's life was made, *Heart Like a Wheel*. The film shows Shirley as a teenager, drag racing on an abandoned country road, where she discovers the thrill of racing speed. And the film deals with the problems of a young woman in a male-only sport. Shirley says that she is still the only woman on the professional drag racing circuit.

How did Shirley go from being a kid driving on the back streets to being one of the top racers in the world? More than anything else it has been the desire to win, along with natural ability and courage. Shirley Muldowney has great determination. She says, "I do not want to lose, either for myself or for my crew—they work so hard to make me do as well as I do. . . . Call me anything you want, but winning says it all."

GLOSSARY
ap·pre·**hen**·sion—fear
cour·age—being very brave, not afraid
de·**sire**—wanting something very much
de·ter·min·**a**·tion—deciding very strongly to do something
drag car—special kind of car for racing
pay at·**ten**·tion to—listen carefully to
thrill—excitement

1. **True or false? For each sentence below, write on your paper *true* or *false*. Be ready to find the evidence to support your answer in the reading. If a sentence is false, write it correctly to make it true.**
    a. Shirley Muldowney is very worried about what other people say and think.
    b. She has been interested in cars since she was very young.
    c. She won the Winston World Championship three times.
    d. She is braver than many men.
    e. The film, *Heart Like a Wheel*, shows how easy it is to be a woman race car driver.
    f. Winning is the most important thing for Shirley.

2. **Answer these questions on your paper.**
    a. How long has Shirley been racing cars?
    b. How long has she been racing professionally?
    c. When did she become the first woman to break the six second barrier?
    d. Are there many professional drag racing women?

3. **Take notes from the passage about imporant facts and dates. Then practice telling your partner a summary of the reading. Finally write a paragraph summarizing the reading in your own words.**

Writing

Answer these questions on your paper. Then discuss them with your partner.

a. How do you think Shirley Muldowney is different from other women? How is she different from other people, men and women?
b. Do you know anyone who has the determination to win and courage like Shirley? Can you describe that person?
c. Have you ever felt that winning something is the most important thing in the world? Tell about that time. What happened?

Listening

Listen to the interview. Answer the questions on your paper.

1. What's the name of the person being interviewed?
2. What's his profession?
3. Where was he born?
4. Where does he live now?
5. When did he start singing?
6. How long has he been singing?
7. What's his favorite song?
8. Why?
9. Where will he go on his next tour?
10. What city will he visit first in Europe?

Writing

Use your answers to the questions above to write a short paragraph about the person being interviewed.

Practice Points

1. **Copy and complete these sentences. Use *have/has* with the correct form of the word in parentheses.**

    a. I (live) here since 1993.
    b. You (watch) TV for more than two hours.
    c. Carlos (wait) for Barbara for half an hour.
    d. Mr. and Mrs. Day are tired because they (work) in the garden since 10:00.
    e. Nell Chambers (drive) professionally since 1992.
    f. Brian Keats (work) for Paramount Records since 1993.
    g. Giorgio (study) English for five years and now he can speak English very well.
    h. I (do) nothing all day but I'm tired anyway.
    i. I (listen) to you for 10 minutes and I still don't understand.
    j. I (read) poetry for years but I've never written any.

2. **Complete these sentences with *for* or *since*.**

    a. We've been waiting for her . . . nine o'clock.
    b. I haven't seen him . . . three months.
    c. He has been in Boston . . . February.
    d. They have been living on that street . . . five years.
    e. Nobody has telephoned me . . . yesterday morning.
    f. He kept asking me the same question . . . more than five minutes.
    g. It has been raining . . . the whole month.
    h. They have been dancing to rock music . . . two hours.
    i. She has been wearing the same old dress . . . last Tuesday.

Let's Rock!

Turn to page 132.
Listen to the song *Rock and Roll Baby*.
Read the words as you listen. Then sing along!

Check Points

Communication Points

Ask and talk about people's lives

How long have you been living in New Jersey?
Well, I've been living there since 1990.
Before that I lived in Philadelphia.
So you've been living there for . . . years.

Ask and talk about past habits

Have you ever driven go-carts?
No, I've never driven go-carts in my life.
Well, I used to drive go-carts, but I don't do that anymore.
Yes, I have. And I still drive go-carts.

1.

| How long | have | you | been | living in . . . ? |
| | has | he she | | racing? |

2.

| I've He's She's | been | living there racing driving | for ten years. since 1992. |

3.

| Have you ever | drunk milk before going to bed? driven go-carts? played with dolls? |

4.

| No, I've never | drunk milk before going to bed driven go-carts played with dolls | in my life. |

5.

| Well, I used to Yes, I have. And I still | drink milk before going to bed. drive go-carts. play with dolls. |

Words and Expressions

anymore	dolls	lollipop	question
anyway	fairy tale	move	race
attend	go-carts	nobody	still
dating	join	poetry	whole
diary	license	professionally	winner

Present	Past	have/has +
drink	drank	drunk
drive	drove	driven
keep	kept	kept
meet	met	met
speak	spoke	spoken
	was born	

Let's Rock!
Song Lyrics

Unit 1

Feelings and Emotions

Words and Music by Bob Schneider

Chorus:
Feelings, emotions
Got so many feelings, like waves upon the ocean.
Feelings, emotions
Got so many feelings, like waves upon the ocean.

It makes me happy when I'm singing with my friends,
Talk about feelings, talk about emotions
Oh, so happy, want to do it again,
Talk about feelings, talk about emotion
It makes me angry when my mama pulls on me.
Talk about feelings, talk about emotion
Oh, so angry I want to climb a tree
Talk about feelings, talk about emotion

Chorus

It makes me sad when my friends all go away,
Talk about feelings, talk about emotion
Oh, so sad, I wish that they could stay,
Talk about feelings, talk about emotion
It makes me shy when I'm in a new place
Talk about feelings, talk about emotion
Oh, so shy, I want to hide my face
Talk about feelings, talk about emotion

Chorus

© 1986 by Schorn Publishing

Unit 2

Going on Vacation

Words and Music by Bob Schneider

Chorus:
Take me to the bus.
Take me to the station.
Take me far away 'cause I'm going on vacation.
Going to see my friends, going to have a celebration,
'cause always feels great when I'm going on vacation.
Going on vacation, going to vacation land.
Going on vacation, going to vacation land.

Sometimes I work, sometimes I work,
Sometimes I play, sometimes I play.
Sometimes I go, sometimes I go on a holiday, on a holiday.
I may go to the East, go to the East.
I may go to the West, go to the West,
Wherever I go, wherever I go it's always the best,
it's always the best. So...

Chorus

I may go the Riviera, By the Mediterranean Sea,
Or down to Jamaica, See the coconut tree.
Or maybe go to Brazil, South American way,
Or over to Australia, where the kangaroos play. So...

Chorus

I may go to California, Lie in the sun.
Or up to the North Pole, where the polar bears run.
Or maybe go to Japan, And speak some Japanese,
Or over to Switzerland, to see the evergreen trees. So...

© 1986 Schorn Publishing

Unit 5

Over and Over Again

Words and Music by Bob Schneider

Verse 1:
From the first time I met you I could never forget you.
I'll always see the smile in your eyes.
So many faces, Beautiful faces,
You always gave me the very best time.

Chorus:
It was over and over again,
we shared a dream.
Over again, over and over again,
we shared a dream, without an end.

Bridge:
Now all of the time—we spend together,
Singing our song melody.
Never quite knowing where it would lead us.
But look at us now,
We're standing proud, And we did it together,
We can sing it forever,
Sing it together, forever my friends!

Verse 1, Chorus

Verse 2:
The first time I saw you I really adored you.
How could I feel anything but love?
Singing our songs we were laughing along,
Sharing feelings, so many feelings,
When we were together, just singing our songs.

Chorus, Bridge, Chorus

© 1986 Schorn Publishing

Unit 8

Street Beat

Words and Music by Bob Schneider

Verse 1:
Kids playing on the sidewalk.
It's the street beat!
All the neighbors just a-talk, talk, talk.
It's the street beat!
Cars and buses make their sounds,
and the policeman is just a-dancing around.
Ev'rybody just a-walking downtown.
It's the street beat! The street beat!

Chorus:
'Cause it's the street beat! And it's the street beat!
Oh, it's the street beat!
It's the street beat! The street beat!

Bridge:
A street beat makes you feel all right.
Feel it ev'ry day, Feel it in the night.
Street beat is all around,
You can feel it ev'ry day in the big city sound

Verse 2:
Playing ball in the alleyway, it's the street beat!
Sirens ringing all night and day, it's the street beat!
The song playing on the radio,
And the crowds of people just a-go-go-go,
If you've got the time come on and join the show,
'Cause it's the street beat!

Chorus, Bridge

Verse 3:
All the boys try to act so cool, it's the street beat!
Oh, when the girls come a-strutting out of school, it's the street beat!
Hanging out at the corner store,
And the grocery man, he comes a-bopping through the door,
Everybody wanting more, more, more,
'Cause it's the street beat!

Chorus

© 1986 Schorn Publishing

Unit 9

Busy, Busy, Busy

Words and Music by Bob Schneider

Chorus:
Deedle-eedle, eedle-eedle, eedle-eedle, ee,
Deedle-eedle, eedle-eedle, eedle-eedle, ee
Busy, busy, busy, busy, busy all the time.
Makes me feel so dizzy when I'm busy all the time!
Busy, busy, busy, busy, busy all the time.
Puts me in a tizzy when I'm busy all the time!
Deedle-eedle, eedle-eedle, eedle-eedle, ee,
Deedle-eedle, eedle-eedle, eedle-eedle, ee!

Verse 1:
Got to do my math, busy all the time.
Got to take a bath, busy all the time.
Go to talk on the phone, busy all the time.
Got to get my dog a bone, busy all the time.
Got to wash the dishes, busy all the time.
Got to feed the fishes, busy all the time.
Got to clean my room, busy all the time.
Got to sweep it with a broom

Bridge:
(Spoken)
Now bow to your partner,
Bow to your corner,
Bow to your mops, your dust pans and brooms

Take your mops and take your brooms,
Going to have a hoe down in this room.
Take the broom up in your hand,
Sweep it in the dustpan if you can.
Sweep it to the left, sweep it to the right,
Sweep that dirt right out of sight.
Promenade around the floor,
Take that broom and sweep some more.
Sweep it to the left, sweep it to the right,
Sweep that dirt right out of sight!

(Spoken)
Now do-si-do your partners,
Do-si-do your corners,
Do-si-do your mops, your dust pans, your brooms,
Anything you like . . .

Chorus, Verse 1, Chorus

Verse 2:
Got to mop the floor, busy (etc.)
Got to paint the door, busy (etc.)
Got to wash my clothes, busy (etc.)
Got to wipe my nose, busy (etc.)
Got to use the vacuum, busy (etc.)
Got to clean the living room, busy (etc.)
Got to mow and hoe, busy (etc.)
Got to do-si-do...

Chorus, Bridge, Chorus

© 1986 Schorn Publishing

Unit 10

No, No, No
Words and Music by Bob Schneider

Verse 1:
Shelley, Shelley, Shelley, got tickets to the show!
No, no, no, don't want to go.
Shelley, Shelley, Shelley, they're in the front row!
Maybe, maybe, baby, I don't really know.
Shelley, Shelley, Shelley, the band is the best!
Yes, Yes, Yes, Oh, what a mess!
Things can be so crazy when you can't make up your mind!
I said, No, no, no, Don't want to go.
Maybe, maybe, maybe, Don't really know.
Yes, yes, yes, Oh, what a mess!
Things can be so crazy when you can't make up your mind!

Chorus:
No, no, no, Don't want to go.
Maybe, maybe, maybe, Don't really know.
Yes, yes, yes, Oh, what a mess!
Things can be so crazy when you can't make up your mind!

Verse 2:
Kerry, Kerry, Kerry, want to go to the game?
No, no, no, don't want to go.
Kerry, Kerry, Kerry, your favorite team is playing!
Maybe, maybe, baby, I don't really know.
Kerry, Kerry, Kerry, the team is the best!
Yes, yes, yes, Oh, what a mess!
Things can be so crazy when you can't make up your mind!

Chorus

Verse 3:
Anna, Anna, Anna, want to go to school?
No, no, no, don't want to go.
Anna, Anna, Anna, the teacher's really cool!
Maybe, maybe, baby, don't really know.
Anna, Anna, Anna, the kids are the best!
Yes, yes, yes, Oh, what a mess!
Things can be so crazy when you can't make up your mind!

© 1986 Schorn Publishing

Unit 12

Weekend

Words and Music by Bob Schneider

Verse 1:
The weekend comes every week
We love it, we love, oh, we really love it.
Saturday, Sunday, Oh, what a treat!
We love it, we love it, oh, we really love it!
Now the weekend makes you feel so fine,
We love it, we love it, oh, we really love it!
Saturday, Sunday, when you're mine, all mine.
Oh,

Chorus:
Playing on the weekend, playing with my friends,
Playing on the weekend, hope it never ends.
Playing on the weekend, morning, noon, and night.

Verse 2:
Now the weekend makes you feel all right.
We love it, we love it, oh, we really love it.
Saturday, Sunday, even Friday night,
We love it, we love it, oh, we really love it.
(etc.)

Chorus

© 1986 Schorn Publishing

Unit 16

Rock and Roll Baby

Words and Music by Bob Schneider

Chorus:
Rock and roll!
Rock and roll!

Verse 1:
Well, a rock and roll baby,
I was born,
rocking in the night and in the early morning.
I remember rocking on my mama's knee.
Well, she rocked, rocked, rocked me to sleep,
A rock-a-bye baby, rocking to the beat!
Hey, Mama, this baby can rock and roll!

Verse 2:
I was a rock and roll baby when I went to school,
Wearing my shades, looking real cool, you know.
I remember rocking almost every day,
Well, I'd rock in the halls, rock in the line,
Rock in the schoolyard all the time.
Hey, mama, this baby can rock and roll!

Chorus

Verse 3:
Now I'm a rock and roll baby to this very day,
I'll keep rocking 'cause I was born that way.
I still remember rocking on my mama's knee,
And I'll keep rocking till the day I die.
I'll even be rocking up in the sky.
Hey, mama, this baby can rock and roll!

Chorus

© 1986 Schorn Publishing

Words and Expressions

Words and Expressions

Number names and irregular verbs follow the expressions at the end of this list. Numbers refer to the units in which words and expressions are introduced.

accept	12	deliver	9	jeans	4
activities	10	design	9	jewelry	9
amusement park	10	diary	16	job	7
anymore	16	diced	8	join	16
anyone	15	discover	9	journalist	9
anyway	16	dish	8	juice	2
architect	9	dolls	16	knife	12
around	3	drain	8	language	7
arrange	12	drawings	2	later	2
attend	16	dress	4	lettuce	8
aunt	3	dressing room	8	license	16
author	9	easy	13	lightly	8
babysitter	9	ever	14	lollipop	16
bacon	2	excited	1	loud	7
badly	12	exciting	6	loudly	11
bear	2	exercise	1	machine	12
before	2	fabulous	7	mad	1
behind	2	fairy tale	16	mail carrier	9
begin	1	fill	8	many	1
belt	4	firefighter	12	maple syrup	8
best	7	fishing rod	3	marmalade	8
better	6	flakes	8	medium	8
between	2	folk-singer	9	men	2
birthday	1	folk song	9	meter	5
blouse	4	French toast	8	mine	3
boil	8	fridge	8	more	6
boots	2	funny	7	most	7
bored	10	games	7	move	16
boring	6	garlic powder	8	much	5
bottle	9	gloves	3	must	2
box	2	go-carts	16	myself	12
boys	1	gold	6	neither	14
break	1	grapefruit	8	new	1
brilliant	7	grated	8	nice	6
bug	1	ground	8	nightlife	7
burn	12	ground beef	8	nobody	16
bus terminal	12	gymnastics	15	noisy	13
buttermilk	8	ham	8	nothing	8
camper	2	handsome	7	number	12
carrots	9	happy	1	nurse	9
cereal	8	hear	1	ours	3
chocolate	8	height	5	ourselves	12
choose	7	hers	3	outside	12
circle	12	herself	12	pancakes	8
circus	14	himself	12	pants	3
control	12	honey	8	partner	6
cool	7	housework	9	peanuts	9
corn	8	ice skate	13	pepper	8
could	10	inch	5	photo	2
countryside	6	incredible	7	playground	1
cousin	2	instead	8	pocket	9
cross	1	interesting	6	poetry	16
cumin seed	8	introduce	12	poultry	8
dairy products	8	island	7	power	1
dangerous	6	itself	12	practice	15
dating	16	jacket	4	professionally	16
delicious	6	jam	8	promise	12

WORDS AND EXPRESSIONS 135

purses	4	skirt	4	turn on	11
question	16	skyscrapers	7	t-shirt	4
quiet	6	slides	5	uncle	2
race	16	sneakers	4	uncovered	8
rare	8	socks	3	under	3
recently	15	special	12	until	3
relatives	15	square	10	vase	11
ring	1	still	16	valuable	6
roller coaster	14	strawberries	8	waterskiing	1
safe	6	subject	2	well done	8
sandals	4	sun	1	went off	1
sausage	8	sweatshirt	4	which	12
scared	1	swimming pool	12	while	1
scrambled	8	taco shells	8	whole	16
scream	1	tape	12	whose	3
seasonings	8	taxi	9	wild	7
shirt	4	teenager	9	win	7
shoes	3	tent	3	winner	16
shorts	4	tests	13	women	2
should	12	than	5	worried	1
shower	1	theirs	3	worse	6
shredded	8	themselves	12	would	8
sidewalk	1	tie	4	wrong	2
silver	6	toast	8	yours	3
simmer	8	tower	10	yourself	12
since	5	try on	8	yourselves	12
size	5	turn off	11		

Expressions

Are you sure?	3
hardly ever	2
I bet	1
I'd rather	13
I don't feel well	13
I'm afraid that	12
in front of	3
in the whole world	8
I sure was	1
last night	1
last summer	1
look after	12
make it 10 o'clock	12
more than anything	8
number one favorite	8
Really?	7
sounds great	12
spend an afternoon	10
start with	8
take care of	9
What happened…?	12

Number Names
Ordinals:

1st to 31st

Irregular Verbs

Present	Past	have/has +
am/is/are	was were	been
begin	began	
break	broke	
buy	bought	bought
cut	cut	cut
do	did	done
drink	drank	drunk
drive	drove	driven
eat	ate	eaten
go	went	gone
grow	grew	grown
have/has	had	
hear	heard	
keep	kept	kept
meet	met	met
read	read	read
ring	rang	
see	saw	seen
speak	spoke	spoken
tell	told	
think	thought	
win	won	
write	wrote	written

Passive Past
was born

Appendix

Words and expressions introduced in Turning Points 1 & 2.

a
accident
add
address
Afghan
afternoon
again
airline
airmail
airplane
airport
all
almost
alone
along
alphabet
always
am
American
an
and
ankle
answer
any
anybody
anything
anywhere
apartment
apple
appointment
are
arm
armchair
arrival
arrive
art
article
at
attendant
attractive
automobile
average
away
backache
bad
baked
ball
banana
bank
barber
baseball
basketball
bat
bathroom
batter
be
beach
beans

beard
beautiful
because
bed
bedroom
bedside table
beef
behind
bench
beside
between
bicycle
big
bike
bird
blonde
board
book
bookshelves
bottom
bowl
bread
breakfast
breast of chicken
bring
broiled
broken
brother
brush
builder
building
bus
bus stop
but
butter
buttered
buy
cafeteria
cake
call (on phone)
camera
campsite
can
Canadian
canaries
can't
car
card
cards
carrot
cartoons
cassette recorder
cat
caught
CD
CD player
cent
chair

change
cheap
check
checkers
cheese
cheesecake
chess
chess pieces
chicken
children
chilled
Chinese
church
cider
city
class
classical music
clean
clock
closet
clothes
cloudy
club
coffee
coffee shop
cola
cold
collect
color
come
comedies
comfortable
comics
computer programmer
concert
cookies
cool
cost
country
cover
cream
cup
curly
cut
Dad
dance
dancer
daughter
day
dentist
departure
desk
dessert
detective stories
detergent
diamond
did
dime

dining room
dinner
disco
do
doctor
dog
dollar
door
doughnuts
down
downstairs
draw
dresser
drink
drive
drugstore
drums
dry
dryer
ear
early
east
eat
editor
eggs
either
elbow
elevator
else
emergency
empty
end
engineer
English
especially
evening
every
exhibit
expensive
explain
eye
fairly
fall
family
famous
fans
fantastic
far
farmer
fast
fat
father
favorite
feed
feel
fever
(a) few
film

find
fine
finger
finish
first
fish
flat
flight
flour
flower
foggy
folk music
food
foot, feet
football
football field
football game
for
forget
fresh
friends
from
fruit
frying pan
furniture
gallon
garage
gate
German
get
get up
give
glass
glasses
go
goldfish
golfer
good
got up
grandmother
grandparents
grapes
graph
grass
great
grilled
grow
growl
guided tours
guitar
hair
hairdresser
half
hall
hamburger
hamster
hand
happen

hard	last name	neck	plate	sick
hat	late	never	play	side
hate	lawyer	newspaper	played	sign
have	leave	next to	plenty	sing
he	left	nickel	police officer	singer
head	leg	night	pony	single-family house
headache	lemonade	no	popcorn	sirloin steak
heat	lesson	noise	pop music	sister
help	let	north	population	sit
helpful	letter	nose	postcard	skate
her	library	not	poster	ski
here	light	now	post office	slice
here's (here is)	like	o'clock	potato	slowly
he's (he is)	liquid	of	pound (lb.)	small
him	list	office	prefer	snowy
hip	listen	often	present	so
his	liter	oil	private	soccer
hit	live	old	problem	soda
hobby	living room	on	pumpkin	sofa
home	lock	once	put	solve
home run	look	only	puzzle	some
homework	love	onto	quart (qt.)	something
horror films	low	open	quarter	sometimes
hospital	lunch	opposite	quiet	son
hot	magazine	orange juice	radio	soon
hot chocolate	mailbox	organ	rain	sore
hot dogs	main course	other	rainy	soup
hotel	make	our	read	south
house	man	out	ready	space
hundred	me	outside	receptionist	spaghetti
hungry	meal	painter	region	Spanish
hurry	meat	painting	restaurant	speak
hurt	mechanic	park	reporter	speech
husband	meet	park (a car)	rice	spell
I	meeting	parking lot	ride	sports
ice cream	melon	parrot	right	spring
idea	melt	party	road	stadium
I'm (I am)	menu	pass	rock music	stairs
imported	Mexican	past	romantic	stamps
in	mile	pastries	room	start
in advance	milk	pastry	root beer	stay
instrument	milkshakes	pay	run	stayed
interview	Miss	pea	sail	steak
invitation	model	peach melba	salad	stereo
invite	modern	pear	salt	stomachache
is	money	pen	same	stop
it	month	penny	sandwich	stories
Italian	morning	people	say	story
Japanese	motel	pets	school	straight
jazz	mother	phone booth	science	street
jogging	motorcycle	phone number	science fiction	student
joke	mountain	photographer	season	study
just	mouth	piano	second	stupid
kilo	movies	pickles	see	subway station
kilogram	Mr.	picnic	send	sugar
kind	Mrs.	picture	serious	summer
kitchen	museum	pie	she	sunny
knee	mustache	piece	she's (she is)	supermarket
know	my	pilot	ship	supper
lake	mystery	pint	shop	sure
lamp	name	pizza	short	sweater
large	nationality	plane	shoulder	swim
last	near	plant	shrimp cocktail	table

taco
take
talk
tall
tea
teach
teacher
team
teeth
telephone
tell
tennis match
that
the
theater
their
them
there
these
they
thin
think
third
thirsty
this
those
thousand
throat
throw
time
tired
to
today
toe
together
tomato
tomorrow
tongue-twister
tonight
too
tooth
top
touch
town
townhouses
traffic
traffic jam
traffic light
train
travel
truck
trumpet
T-shirt
turn
turn off
turtles
TV
twice
two-family house
typewriter
understand
up
us

use
usually
vacation
van
vanilla
vegetable
very
visit
waist
wait
waiter
wake up
walk
warm
was
wash
washing machine
watch
watched
water
we
wear
weather
week
weekend
welcome
well
went
were
west
western
what's (what is)
when
where
which
white
who
why
wife
window
windy
winter
with
woman
work
worry
write
x-ray
yard
yes
yesterday
yogurt
you
young
your
you're (you are)
zoo

Expressions
a couple of
a friend of mine
all evening
all right
a lot of fun
Anything else?
as usual
At last!
Bye!
Bye, you guys!
Can I help you?
Can you do me a favor?
Come in.
Come on!
Don't worry.
do the dishes
Excuse me.
Gee . . .
Good afternoon.
Good-bye
Good evening.
Good morning.
Good night.
Great!
Great idea!
Happy Birthday!
Have a good time!
Hello!
Here I am.
Here you are.
Hey, look!
Hey, you guys!
Hi!
Hold on a minute.
How about . . . ?
How about you?
How are you?
How big . . . ?
How do you do?
How far . . . ?
How many . . . ?
How much?
How much is it all together?
How nice.
How old are you?
Hurry up!
I'd/you'd/he'd/she'd/we'd/they'd better . . .
I'd like some .. .
I don't know.
I don't think so.
I'm a little . . .
I'm broke.
I'm free on . . .
I mean . . .
I must hurry now.
I'm not too young . . .
I'm sorry.

in fact
I see.
Is that it?
It's pretty far
Keep your eye on the ball.
Let me know in advance
Let's go.
Let's go/get . . .
Let's go look at it.
Let's have a look.
Let's see . . .
Look at him go!
looks like
lots of
Make the bed.
My pleasure
never mind
Nice to meet you.
No kidding!
No problem.
No, thanks.
Nothing special.
Not very well, I'm afraid
of course
Oh, gosh!
Oh, I see.
Oh, my gosh!
Oh, really?
Oh, sure.
Oh, thanks.
Okay
Over there . . .
Please
. . ., right?
right now
see you . . .
See you later.
See you soon.
See you tomorrow.
. . . , sir.
so long
spare time
strike out
Take care!
thanks
Thanks a lot.
Thank you.
That's a pity.
That sounds super!
That's right.
That's too bad.
They're something else!
Wait a minute
Watch out!
Watch TV
What about . . . ?
What are you doing?
What can I do for you?

What else?
What's it like?
What's wrong with her/him?
What time is it?
Well, . . .
Why don't we . . . instead?
Wouldn't you know?
Wow!
Yes, I do.
Yes, please.
You can't miss it.
You do?
You're right.
You're up!
You're welcome.

Number Names
1–12, 13–23
30–90, 100–999
1,000 and above

Color Names
black   green   red
blue   orange white
brown   pink   yellow

Days   Months

Irregular Verbs

Present	Past
am/is/are	was/were
catch	caught
come	came
do	did
drink	drank
drive	drove
eat	ate
forget	forgot
get	got
go	went
have	had
hit	hit
pay	paid
see	saw
send	sent
sit	sat

Photo Credits

Page 4, Associated Press Photos / Altemdro Nunes; Page 8, (a) New York Convention and Visitors Bureau, (b) Redwood Empire Association, (c,e) Janet Muller, (d) Berg & Associates / Henry D. Meyer, (f) Swiss National Tourist Office; Pages 18–19, Sportschrome East/West, © Brian Drake; Page 31, George Mastellone; Page 34 (L) Gene Shaw / Star File Photo, (R) Dominick Conde / Star File Photo; Page 40 (L) New York Public Library, Rare Books and Manuscript Division / Astor, Lenox, and Tilden Foundations, (R) New York Convention and Visitors Bureau; Pages 46, 48, Movie Star News; Page 51, New York Convention and Visitors Bureau; Page 58 (Top) George Mastellone, (Center) Mary Messenger, (Bottom) Berg & Associates / Arnold Kaplan; Page 63, George Mastellone; Page 64 (Top L) National Aeronautics and Space Administration, (Top C) Redwood Empire Association, (Top R) New York Convention and Visitors Bureau, (Bottom L) John Wilson; Page 65, (Top L) © Stephen Frisch / Stock Boston, (Top R) © Catherine Carnow / Woodfin Camp & Associates, Inc., (Center) Bob Daemmrich / Stock Boston, (Bottom L) Jeff Dunn / Stock Boston, (Bottom C) Lawrence Migdale / Stock Boston, (Bottom R) Gerd Ludwig / Woodfin Camp & Associates, Inc.; Page 72, Central Office of Information, London; Pages 82–83, Associated Press / Wide World Photos; Page 88, (Top L) William Gibbons, (Top R), Ralph Turcotte; Page 89, (a,b) Claire Smith, (c,d,e,g) William Gibbons, (f) Ralph Turcotte, (h/bottom) George Mastellone; Pages 91–92, Courtesy of Ringling Brothers Barnum and Bailey Combined Shows, Inc.; Page 97, (Top, Bottom) March Tuschman, (Center) Boston Museum of Science; Page 107, © Jim Anderson 1984 / Woodfin Camp & Associates, Inc.; Pages 118–119, Leslie Lovett / NHRA.

Poetry Credits

Pages 13, 53 from *Class Dismissed II* by Mel Glenn. Text copyright © 1986 by Mel Glenn. Reprinted by permission of Clarion Books / Houghton Mifflin Co. All rights reserved.

Page 37, from *I Feel the Same Way* by Lilian Moore. Copyright © 1967 by Lilian. Reprinted by permission of Marian Reiner for the author.